MEDITATIONS OF A SPORTSMAN
By Richard Morris

Reflections On Sport, Spirituality, Life.

*"Most men think more about sport than sex.
Most women's thoughts are more wide ranging."*

First published by Lulu.com

Copyright © Richard Morris Publishing 2012

Richard Morris Publishing
richardmorris12@talktalk.net

Book Design by The Fantastics

First Edition
ISBN: 978-1-4717-1945-5

All Rights Reserved.

"Most men think more about sport than sex
Most women's thoughts are more wide ranging."

Richard Morris has had a varied career apart from his sporting successes. Born in Wimbledon he has lived in London all his life. He attended St Olaves and St Saviours Grammar School in Bermondsey where he gained three" O" Levels. A series of jobs from which he got dismissed or stomped out of included being on the ground staff at Charlton Athletic, a builder's labourer, a shop assistant and The Office of National Statistics. He became the proprietor of an antique business for 26 years, then a London Blue Badge Guide, Parliament and York Minster Guide and Tour manager. He gained a BA through the Open University and an MA Literature and Politics through Roehampton University. For over ten years he was an Adult Education Lecturer for Wandsworth Borough Council specialising in History, Beliefs and The History Of London. For one year he was a mentor to a boy with Asperger's Syndrome at local school Swaffield Primary where he eventually became the Drama and Cricket director. He wrote and directed his own children's plays which are successfully published on www.lazybeescripts.co.uk

He also worked as a volunteer for the homeless at St Mungo's, Waterloo, running a play writing group and at Bonny Downs Community Centre in East Ham where he did drama with children and ran a writing group for the over fifties. Whilst working as a volunteer for East London Heritage Oral history project, he was commissioned by The Lord Mayor's office to write a community play for Drew School, My Silver Town, My Silver Town. He wrote Grace Under Pressure which was chosen as a Critic's Choice by TimeOut and played to sold out houses at The Old Red Lion in Islington. Bitter Fruit Of Palestine at Baron's Court got slammed by the Times critic which he regards as a badge of honour. Richard then adapted Bitter Fruit into a monologue which he performed in Oxford and London and is now on YouTube and Vimeo.com. Currently Richard writes a blog wallsofdespair.blogspot.com. His other blog is richardmorrisplaywright.blogspot.com

For Karen

I dedicate this book to Karen who has never wavered in her love and support for my endeavours. She has also helped edit and read the book for errors of syntax and grammar and made useful criticisms of its content. Not the least of it, she has listened to my endless cries for help and reassurance. All errors are my responsibility.

I owe massive thanks to the brave friends who read and commented on the book in progress. David Solomon, a dear friend who has read most of my work before publication or performance. Roger Tredre, author of a book on Fashion and my nephew, a fellow suffering England supporter. Tessa, my daughter, a fellow writer with powers of succinct and sharp observations.

From the side lines thanks to Sophie and Gary for always taking an interest in the novel and for all the love they shower on us. For the "Frenchies" whose generous hospitality and friendship is always a pleasure.

Very special thanks to wearethefantastics.com the talented creative graphic and film duo of Peter Willment and Nick Smith who are responsible for the illustrations in the book and for the final publishing and layout of the book.

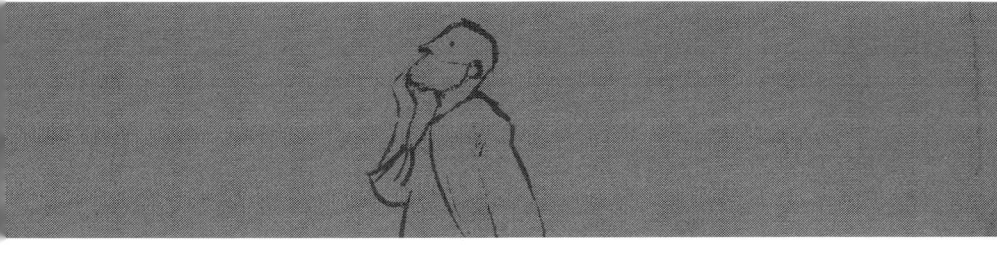

Prologue
Have I Already Told You This?

I woke up in the year 2010 and didn't know where I was;
Gusts of wind and rain agitated against the windowpane.
Was it winter, summer, autumn, or spring?
The central heating cranked into life.
Must be Winter.
Muzzy headed, staring into the darkness, I could make out the shape of Rosy the cat, her head tucked under one paw, snoring gently in the hollow of my pillow, her whiskers twitching in time, a paw brushing my cheek, so maybe it was Wandsworth; a refuge of idiosyncratic cats and equally odd humans.
It was not, I decided, my beloved Suffolk of divine sunsets and country smells. I still had my earphones on with a Bassoon Concerto by Mozart announced by Sara Mohr Pesch. I didn't even know Wolfgang Amadeus Mozart had ever written anything for the bassoon. I think he must have been composing in the womb and came fully sprung into the world with melodies swirling and prancing through his dancing, fertile brain.
My throat was dry and my lower back painful. My atrial fibrillation was speeding away and my pulse racing to keep up. I reached out and found the metal pill box.
I swallowed the first of my ration of life preserving pills for the day.
An ominous note reverberated in my mind.
Was this it, time to go? Had I missed the angels' roll call?
Where was the ambulance?
These days, if an ambulance pulls up in the street I just get in.
I suddenly got severe cramp in my calf and a searing pain down the other leg. My vivid dreams leapt from my mind, gone in a flash for ever as I eased the leg

downwards to relieve the cramp and sweat broke out on my forehead. What had I delved into during the watching hours of the night?

Where had I been?

Had I dreamt I was in my seventies or was I in my eighties?

Was I in an institution for the forgetful or was I at home being cared for by legions of big bosomed nurses, smiling and cooing whilst jabbing medication into my arms or pouring pills down my throat? I hurt in every area of my overweight body; my knees are like solid concrete, my arms unable to rise above my shoulders.

I move in stages towards the bathroom, holding on to landmarks to steady myself.

Has that chair always been there? Who put this stool on the landing?

I stub my toe and curse.

I take a wrong turn, grope for the light, finally gain the sanctuary of the lavatory hoping against hope I will be able to pee, having spent the best part of the night waiting, waiting for something to trickle into the pan.

Lo and behold it arrives in a pleasing stream and I have got through the first hurdle of the day.

I look in the mirror and don't recognise the wild eyed gargoyle staring back, hair sticking up like Worzel Gummidge.

My eyes are dripping pus, the boil on my bum eating into my skin and my mind.

What happened last night? Had I spent the evening in the garden sipping wine and sampling three different cheeses, the best one a creamy, crusty Camembert washed down finally by an ancient port.

Karen and I laughing like gurgling drains about times remembered. Sophie and Tessa, my daughters returning from a night out and making us laugh all over again with their stories.

Fanciful, erotic, hopeful, despairing dreams inhabit a portion of the territory of my mind. The rest is a wasteland of repetition.

I draw back my arm and execute the perfect forehand volley.

I go down on one knee and drive gloriously; a hard red ball races through the covers. The crowd roars, and the Ashes are ours.

I weave, I feint, and I strike. The net ripples, the ball spirals up the back of the net.

I turn, arms raised in triumph as men and women weep and multi coloured scarves cascade upon my head.

I dream of a hot pavement in a hot country. My feet are bleeding; my mind is numb as I enter the stadium after twenty six miles. I see a podium of gold. I wearily climb the stairs.

The anthem rings out, the flag climbs the pole. I wipe away the tears.

My medal bangs against my chest.

Of such stuff…

The only constant in my life is recurring nightmares; torrents pouring down my mind. Why can't I reach my destination? What is my destination? I'm lost, lost.

Strangers turn away when I ask for directions. Why has the train already gone, the plane left the tarmac, the coach sped away on the motorway?

Questions: Is there anyone there?

Who are these people crowding around my prone body?

What traitors' questions are; stealing into our minds day and night, wraithlike and insidious, unwilling, unable to display their ugliness?

It is written that everything comes to an end. Or is it?

Where is it written? How does it happen? Why does it come to pass?

What are the choices?

Shall I live and die in a world of narrow incomprehension, never seeking, never asking questions or should I stay curious to the end? Can I stay curious to the end?

In the face of adversity my frustrations boil over because everything is down to referees, umpires, penalties and injuries. Will it be the malevolent or benign Gods hawking their wares to alleviate, destroy or advance my dreams and fantasies.

Che sara Che sara?

An image of Doris Day swam into view.

Whatever will be, will be.

Many of us strive for beauty, for harmony, proportion and splendour, mentally building an architectural masterpiece or a lasting memorial in art or literature. Beauty is in the eye of the beholder.

Socrates the philosopher was notoriously ugly but possessed a mind of such magnitude he appeared as handsome.

"Beauty is a short lived tyranny ".

"As for me, all I know is that I know nothing."

Walking in the agora in Athens and seeing the plethora of goods he asked "What do I need?"

Helen of Troy's face launched a thousand ships.

Hugh of Fouilly wrote in the thirteenth century that women's breasts should protrude but little and be moderately full, restrained but not compressed, gently bound so that they are not free to jounce about.

The love of male beauty sent Oscar Wilde to Reading Jail and the tyranny of the treadmill. Wilde then wrote one of the most hostile, beautiful and moving love letters in history from prison which he titled De Profundis, addressed to the treacherous, weak and pretty Lord Alfred Douglas. He wrote of his distress and shame but also wrote "where there is sorrow there is holy ground." His close and loyal friend Robert Ross stood amongst the jeering crowd in the corridor of the Bankruptcy Court so that,

"He might gravely raise his hat to me. Men have gone to heaven for smaller things than that." I thought of Wilde's striving to the end for le mot juste, the witty riposte. His last words were reportedly spoken from his bed in the Hotel d'Alsace in Paris.

"My wallpaper and I are fighting a duel to the death. One or other of us has to go."

For the dead of the First World War the poet Laurence Binyon wrote,

"Age shall not wither them nor the years condemn,

At the going down of the sun and in the evening we shall remember them."

We shall remember them; thousands of them.

Beautiful young men and women trapped for ever in sepia photographs and grainy film, fresh faced and smiling as they marched off to sodden fields of doom and muddy death. *Keep the Home Fires Burning* they sang. *There'll Be A Welcome In the Hillsides, It's A Long Way To Tipperary, Good Byee; don't Cryee.*

But what of the survivors gasping out their last days laden with medals and lacerating memories, trapped in wheelchairs being pushed towards the charnel house?

Oh What A Lovely War.

Is this all there is?

Lately my philosophy has let me down. I seem to be holding off from facing the final curtain, of kicking the bucket, of being brown bread, of popping off, counted out, lately of this parish. I worry about my wobbly mind like Harriet Beecher Stowe did as she grew older; "my mental condition might be called nomadic. Now and then I dip into a book much as a humming bird, poised on whirring wing darts into the heart of a flower… nowhere then there and away."

I have, I think my moments. Just wish I was there when they happened.

In my mind I rehearse my own funeral. A traditional jazz band is waiting outside the house. It sets off playing a slow tempo, the musicians singing,

"Ashes to ashes, dust to dust, if the women don't get you the whisky must."
"Didn't He ramble! Didn't He ramble!
He rambled 'til the butchers cut him down"

The trumpet and clarinet soar as the tempo increases and moves into marching music. We move forward, me in my best black rollneck jumper, brown trousers with an expanding waistband and my brown belt with the false brass buckle bought from the Market in Chania, Crete thirty years ago.

My very old but cherished herringbone overcoat bought for £300 in Aquascutum forty years ago. My Groundwork boots, the mud washed off by Karen, complete the ensemble.

I lie, my white hair overflowing my collar in a cardboard casket, on a black and silver carriage drawn by two black prancing plumed horses.

As we enter the Chapel of Rest, Elvis is singing *Don't Be Cruel*.

"Dearly beloved we are gathered here today" intones a lady from the Humanist Society. "Richard wanted me to say that," she smiles and the congregation laugh.

Friends read poems by John Clare, Gerald Manley Hopkins and John Donne.

Elgar's *Cello Concerto* played by Jacqueline du Pre sends its plaintive notes into the chapel and many close their eyes to listen to its haunting echoes.

Then, a pause before they hear the sepulchral tones of Leonard Cohen singing *Hallelujah*.

The congregation joins in the chorus.

My daughters talk about me, I hope with affection and humour.

As the coffin slides out for its burning like a Post Office parcel on a conveyor belt, Paul Simon sings *Graceland*. The mourners gaily bedecked in a variety of dress file out and wait in the watery sunshine as the band plays *Just a Closer Walk with Thee*.

In my dreams, a panoramic vision of days of pain and glory flash by, glimpses revealed as if from a speeding train window.

**The End is not Certain.
Lights! Action! Music!
From an original script by Richard Morris
Fade out.**

I've played and prayed, made comebacks. I've wept as my hamstring goes again and I limp from the field. I have hit sixes, scored centuries, taken wickets and catches, created and scored lots of goals. I've won Wimbledon and a World Cup Winners medal; taken part in an Ashes series, run marathons and short sprints.

I have been a hero to the young and old alike. Or have I?

Is this book a meditation, memoir or a novel?

It is up to you to swelter at the task. I can but write write write.

I feel like Gibbon, who having written his epic *The Decline and Fall of the Roman Empire*, met George the Third who asked him,

"Still scribble scribble Mr Gibbon?"

I think maybe all the striving really is coming to an end. The newspapers and magazines I read have become a constant recycling of repetition. People I have never heard of relate their parent's terrible deaths, the loss of a beloved child, friend, a promising career curtailed. Some write of wanting to change their jobs, partners.

We learn yet again of the crisis of youth, the selfishness of the baby boomers.

Those of the elderly who enter the nether world of Alzheimers or being placed in a Home for the terminally ill have their sufferings chronicled by their journalist relatives. The resigned survivors talk or write of their sense of relief, of still having their faculties if not their health.

I am not sure where I am in the pantheon of pain and memory.

I can remember so many of the great sportsmen and women I have met or played with, but I can't remember if I have taken my panaceas of pills.

I can name the British Kings and Queens from 1066 to today and the American Presidents from George Washington to today but I can't recall the name of my doctor or the person in front of me I have known for twenty years.

The old joke about reading the obituaries to check I'm still alive doesn't make me laugh anymore. I have great days when I wisely and succinctly advise others on the vagaries of getting old. Other days when a cold fog descends and I stagger from bookcase to bookcase trying to find a book I definitely know I own but where on earth is it?

I read that life expectancy is becoming longer and longer in the West.

So now I watch and listen to old people on the Common or in the Tube and see how mobile they are, and how they talk. I devour television programmes where decrepit people with shaking heads, withered fingers and unsteady gait insist that the life of the mind compensates for the failures of the body to respond any longer to our commands. I try to explain to friends and family that instead of white haired wisdom lying like a snowy mantle on my shoulders, I have lost confidence, drive and ambition.

The days of clear headed thought and the making of plans for the future are outnumbered by the days of futile contemplation of the future and resignation to the atrophying of my limbs and mind.

Sometimes I feel like Diogenes who when asked why he was talking to a marble statue said,

"I'm practicing disappointment."

Or maybe it's the Marquess of Salisbury, British Prime Minister in 1902 discovered by his wife sleepwalking on a balcony declaiming, "Democracy! Democracy! Keep back. Keep back!"

I am subject like Mathieu in the *Age of Reason* to "long moments of exile."
So what to do or to say?

I'm only trotting out the same clichés as all the rest of the ageing population, the musings that civilians, the professional writers and thinkers bombard us with.

Everything has been said or explored; yet another day, another ailment, another pill.

Sex, drugs and rock and roll are lost in the enveloping mist.

Heavy petting has become heavy patting. Heavy breathing is the result of walking up the stairs, not of erotic activities. I jabber away on a variety of subjects but look around to realise I am being drowned out by a howling tempest where lurk the Furies, ready to cut out my tongue. In a dream I bend the knee and kneel penitent before the Abbot in a dark sombre monastery and take a vow of silence as a Trappist monk but it is all in vain.

I can't resist the avalanche of words that fill the chattering part of my brain, the unceasing round of calls and responses made like monks at the Mass.

Masticated and digested, the disloyal and slippery adjectives, nouns and verbs issue forth as repetitious old stories, reminiscences of my childhood, my growing up, the agonies and the ecstasies of love made and forgotten, the insults given and received, friendships forged for ever and others dropped by the wayside.

Bear with me dear dear readers. Help me. See the other side of my face, the beams of brightness in the dark of the night. Tarry with me awhile in sylvan memories and foolish ambitions and let's see if we can ignore these seasons of distress and grief.

I am going on a progress through the gate marked private, into the sloughs of despair, along muddy and treacherous paths.

Be my comforter, be my friend. Oh we'll have some fun, we always do.

At the stations on the way we'll try to alleviate the pain, to fill the empty void where the gods used to dwell.

You can't be serious!

I don't know.

Am I serious amidst all this frivolity?

When did I first notice my condition?

Part One

"To sleep, perchance to dream." *Shakespeare.*

In the old days "when wits were fresh and clear / And life ran gaily as the sparkling Thames / Before this strange disease of modern life / With its sick hurry, its divided aims.
Malcolm Arnold – The Scholar Gipsy.

I have heard it said that most men think more about sport than sex.

Most women's thought are more wide ranging, I'm told.

Time and again throughout my life sport has permeated my sleeping and waking hours. Somewhere in the great prairie of my mind, I am always driving a red hard leather ball with a wide seam through the covers and raising my bat to acknowledge the applause for my 100th century. At other times I am beating man after man, always on Wembley's hallowed turf to reach the penalty area before crashing the ball, this time a bigger leather ball, into the net.

As I walk on Wimbledon Common I think of the Centre Court just down the road.

I am chasing down an angled shot from Rod Laver and thrash the ball past him.

He grins and cheerfully calls out "Good Shot Mate."

When I walk home from the tube I make bets with myself.

If I reach the lamp post outside the newsagent before any vehicle of any kind has passed then England will win the crucial qualifier tonight.

My dreams are so real that I wake up with my heart beating after exerting myself to win Wimbledon for the record tenth time. I'm constantly waiting for an envelope to drop through the letter box inviting me to a trial, or a phone call asking if I am available for a Test Match.

I can't remember when the obsessive love affair began. I kicked a tennis ball around on the bomb sites near our house or in Greenwich Park with other young kids.

My mother loved to play rounders with us in Greenwich Park on golden summer evenings bringing out orange squash and biscuits to revive our flagging efforts.

The only contact I had with my father was when he came home drunk and forced me to put on boxing gloves.

He was tall and handsome but his face was ravaged, his silver hair plastered in hair cream, his eyes unfocussed and he had the silly lop sided smile of drunks, his row of shining white teeth glinting in the dark of the lounge. I timidly struck at his bloated face, hating every minute of the ritual.

"Hit me, go on hit me. Be a tough guy like your daddy."

He used shoe trees for his immaculate brown brogues and his trousers had sharp creases. His shirts were crisp, the starched collars cutting into his skin, his ties unstained. Flecks of blood were visible on his neck where his unsteady hands had caused the shaving blade to cut too deep. He disappeared for some years from my life before resurfacing at football matches I played in when I could hear his drunken pseudo posh voice crying out, "Go on Richard." Coming home on the bus after a night out with the lads, I would shrink back in my seat as he would climb on the bus from whichever pub he had graced with his presence and say "Take me home Driver."

John Henry Morris, born in Silvertown in 1898 had worked at The Royal Naval College, Greenwich as Resident Engineer and we lived in a terraced house opposite the College and a few hundred yards from Greenwich Park. Before we were evacuated from there to Devon during the Second World War, I can remember the nightly air raids.

The sirens were a long wailing sound that if I hear today persuade vivid memories to come swirling into my mind. "Put out those lights." Whispering adult voices,

"The Kelly's house got it... everybody's gone."

My mother would shake me awake and urge me to put on my slippers and dressing gown. "Wake up Richard; come on there's an air raid warning. We're going to the shelter". The shelter was just across the road next to Greenwich Pier. We went down some concrete steps into a dank smelly cellar. Brown dust covered the benches.

We shuffled along the seats as more people came down, sending up little grains of dust. Some of the women wore hair nets; others had obviously put some lipstick on too hastily. Dogs barked and one lady had her budgerigar in its cage swinging back and forth in the erratic light. The typical banter of the working class volleyed back and forth under which the quaver in the voice revealed the fear and worry for loved ones. Many of the men worked in the West Indies Docks which were a target for the Luftwaffe.

We weren't in Devon for long but long enough as our houses in King William Walk, Greenwich took a bomb hit and were demolished.
Today the Cutty Sark the old tea clipper stands in their place.

On our return an 18th century house in Maze Hill Greenwich owned by the Naval College was offered to us and we lived there until my father's world turned upside down and he exchanged Maze Hill for Pentonville Prison. He had "borrowed" some money from the office safe and had "forgotten" to return it. The house went with the job so we eventually had to move out. James Callaghan the future Prime Minister took our place. Years later when I was a builder's labourer for a time I worked on the house and astonished Mr Callaghan and his wife Audrey by telling them I had lived there and knew how to let myself out from the gate at the back of the garden.

The house had a big garden surrounded by a high brick wall. The back gate opened into Greenwich Park. A large boiler house was at the back with a yard behind it. For a time my mother reared chickens which terrified me and my sister Susan, chasing us around the garden and yard. I kept racing pigeons for a while which came in useful later on in my life.

In the centre of the garden was a famous mulberry tree said to date from the time of Charles the Second which disgorged red fruits every summer that stained my hands, face and feet.

I climbed as high as I dared and sat on a branch and stuffed the mulberries into my mouth until I was sick. My mother put lots of the succulent berries into tightly screwed down glass jars and we had mulberry jam throughout the winter on thick slices of white bread with margarine.

Both the wall and the tree played a big part in my highly successful early sports career. The winter of 1947 was the coldest on record for many years.

I was sent by my mother with the bag wash in a pram and then to the coal merchants to beg for some fuel. Muffled in a scarf and thin coat, wearing gloves, I trudged through the snowy streets thinking of scoring a hat trick for the school and being signed up by Charlton Athletic. I went to the off licence for my father with empty bottles of ale shamefully clinking in the bag and returned with full ones and watched as he got drunk. When our archaic heating system broke down and we had no hot water for the bath I went to Greenwich Baths. An attendant opened a thick mahogany door with a number on it and turned on brass taps which filled a huge white enamel bath to a certain level.

A bar of carbolic soap and a towel were provided. If you felt the water was too tepid you called out, "More hot water in number five please," and as if by magic more water poured into the bath. At home we ate horse and whale meat and sat around a pathetic paraffin lamp and the kitchen stove. Frost covered the windows inside and outside and I used to huddle under the blankets until the last minute before dragging my way to Royal Hill Primary School through Greenwich Park after a breakfast of Quaker Porridge Oats with salt and the top of the cream of the milk, if I was lucky.

The snow lay cold and pristinely beautiful all over the park with only dogs paw prints marking out the paths. The trees sagged with the weight of the snow and I used to pretend to my mother when I got home I was suffering from snow blindness and ought to have the next day off. I loved to make her cry by pretending I was the self-sacrificing Lawrence "Titus Oates" from Scott of the Antarctic. I'd open the back door of the kitchen, put my hand on my heart and say, "I am going out and may not be back for some time." We had seen the film at the local Odeon sitting in the one and nines, a big treat. She had loved the film starring John Mills and we both wept buckets at that scene.

Blessing, my friend from across the road had a wood sledge which we toiled with for hours dragging it up Observatory Hill, the statue of General Wolfe keeping a cold eye on us. He knew about victory, defeat, and false friends. We would compete to see who could get the farthest without pushing with our hands, floating in an ecstatic current of fun and mild hysteria. Other children had trays or bits of wood, no gloves and raw red hands. Afterwards we wrapped our chilled hands around a cup of cocoa and slapped ourselves into some kind of warmth. I felt alive and full of a sense that one day life would be better and that I would love Blessing for ever.

The summer was one long glorious fiesta of sun, rounders and Lyons or Wall's ice cream, Tizer and cricket.

And I became Denis Compton.

I scored over 3,000 runs that summer, my brylcreamed hair glistening in the sun, my charming smile beaming down from billboards all over Britain.

When I scored a century I modestly waved my bat all around the ground and usually got out to the next ball. I was given a new cricket bat for Christmas. Linseed oiled and the handle wrapped in black tape, I practiced in front of the mirror looking at my sports annuals. Walter Hammond was featured in coloured photographs with Jack Hobbs and the founder of the modern game W.G Grace. Depicted and explained in captions, I learnt the Forward defensive stroke, how to drive off the back foot, easily and seemingly without effort to cover drive a four along the ground to the boundary, to cut, glance and hook.

Then I walked out into the garden, transformed into Lords, paced out my run-up from the mulberry tree as Ray Lindwall or Keith Miller and tore in like a whirlwind sending the tennis ball against the wall.

The ball rebounding onto my waiting bat, Denis Compton went down on one knee and crashed the ball through the covers. After reading the sports pages of the News Chronicle, I was Jim Laker artfully spinning England to victory or Alec Bedser in his huge boots pounding in to deliver to the great Don Bradman.

The Don waited quietly for me to run up, patting his bat in the crease, and then carefully and elegantly pushed the ball to the boundary without any apparent effort.

I could block all day like Trevor Bailey and save the game on a sticky wicket.

I could come out to bat with a broken leg or arm, bandaged from head to toe like a First World War soldier, the crowd rising to their feet and applauding me all the way to the pavilion after my match saving seventy two, not out.

I was Eric Hollies when he bowled out Bradman for a duck on his last appearance in England in 1948 which left him with a Test career average of 99.

I almost felt like apologising but choked back the words as he strode back to the pavilion. What moved me was that he had tears in his eyes caused by the standing ovation he had received from the crowd as he came to the wicket. I had bowled him my best googly and often regret I didn't give him at least one loose ball to get off the mark. Four runs and he would have retired with a Test average of one hundred.

I was in my element in 1953 when as Denis Compton I pulled a four to the boundary for England to regain the Ashes, little realising that I was to play a part in a future Ashes series. Later the cricket hours of dreaming were enhanced by the genius and the honour of becoming The Hon Sir Garfield St Aubin Sobers, National Hero of Barbados. This involved some adjustments. Born with two extra fingers I removed them myself with catgut and a sharp knife whilst still a teenager.

I bandaged my fingers after I had completed the operation.

"You okay to bat, Garfield?", grinned the indulgent cricket master.

"Yes Sir," I said through gritted teeth and walked with my gangling bandy legged gait to the wicket to save the game for the school.

I was the first batsman to hit six sixes in an over. The game came easily to me, and my instantly recognisable walk and run-up to the wicket and loose limbed action were eye catching and thrilling to behold as I swooped in from the outfield and returned the ball all in one fluid movement or ambled up to the wicket to bowl medium pacers or spinners.

Batting skills were all in my eye and hand coordination. I "saw" the ball very early.

I was a true sportsman to my fingertips and always "walked."

My other skills were losing a lot of money "on the horses."

In the winters at Maze Hill the door of the boiler house was the goal and I was the Wizard of Dribble, Stanley Matthews. Or I might be Raich Carter or Peter Docherty, either laying on goals for Stanley Mortensen or headers for Tommy Lawton or banging them in from twenty yards as Tom Finney.

I trained as Stanley Mortensen after reading in my Charlie Buchan football annual that he practised by running short ten yard bursts of speed. I tore around the mulberry tree and back to the Boiler House. If it snowed or rained I played in there, the walls resounding to the sound of the ball and my exertions. Some days the applause was deafening and I had to stand and acknowledge it, drink it in and wipe tears from my eyes.

I used to clean a neighbour's car. Mr Croft was a tall lugubrious man with unkempt nostrils and a melancholy face. I later learnt that a beloved daughter had died at a young age. He asked one day in 1950 if I wanted to go to Wembley for the Cup Final.

I can remember the atmosphere as if it was yesterday. We shuffled up Wembley Way with good humoured fans joshing each other about their team's chances, a light warm rain failing to disperse our mood of excitement.

I had never seen such an arena. Flowers of every hue were overflowing from the Royal Box; King George and Queen Elisabeth regally acknowledging the ebullient but respectful crowd. I was strangely moved by the crowd singing *Abide With Me* and everybody standing for the National Anthem. The players seemed a long way off, not like the giants of my scrap book but small stocky figures against the backdrop of multi coloured waving scarves of the fans and the sound of football rattles.

There was a sense of ritual, of togetherness, an appreciation of both side's skills by the fans, a part of sport tarnished and faded today by vulgar and ignorant abuse of opposing fans. The word fan no longer carries the same evocations.

The players and crowd shared the austerity of a Britain, only five years away from the horrors of war and learning more and more about the barbarities of the Nazis and concentration camps. Ration books and coal shortages were forgotten in Wembley's welcoming bowl.

My idol Denis Compton proved his place in the marble halls of immortality by playing top level football and cricket. He played on the left wing for Arsenal but even then I could see he was struggling with his left leg and was a little overweight.

Billy Liddell for Liverpool was another idol pasted many times into my red scrap book which I still have. All wingers "bustled" in those days according to the press but Billy was a direct no frills two footed winger. I treasured his background.

He played for Lochgelly Violet, a mining town in Fife before wartime service as an officer pilot navigator. He trained as an accountant and one of the deals he was offered at Liverpool was as a part time accountant at a firm in the City.

So revered was he at Liverpool by the fans that they called the team Liddellpool.

Denis's brother Lesley played at centre half. "Solid and rocklike" was his description.

He too was a formidable cricketer and kept wicket for Middlesex. He played for Arsenal for 22 years and represented England at 38 years of age.

The Arsenal captain was bandy legged Joe Mercer who later managed Manchester City. Redheaded Archie Forbes "the engine of the team" was right half for Arsenal and Billy Fagan a skilful "scheming" inside right for Liverpool. Arsenal won with two goals from their inside left Reg Lewis. I still have the programme costing one shilling from the day and a mental picture of Lewis's goals. My scrapbook of football was filled with pasted in reports from the newspapers and my own comments.

"Liverpool never really troubled the rock like Arsenal defence" and "Reg Lewis banged his goals home very coolly."

Gods and Monsters

"If you wish to draw tears from me you must first feel pain yourself."
Horace – Ars Poetica.

There are gods who stride through the annals of sport in my mind.
They often fall, stumble, get sick, die young but nothing can take away the effect they had on my young mind. My plastic toy soldiers played football not war, titanic games on the kitchen table culminating in yet another victory for England.
Blessing, my best friend who was what my mother called a half caste walked to school with me.
Her mother Sheila was a headmistress and one of the loveliest persons I ever met, an angel inside and outside her body. Tall and erect with white hair pulled back in a bun, she wore sensible flat brogues, pristine white blouses and tailored blue or grey jackets and skirts. Her big blue eyes seemed to see and understand everything about the difficulties and hazards of being a child. She truly listened when we told her of our fears and hopes. We had instant rapport and she quietly helped to educate me about life and literature. Her bookshelves contained so many books there was a surplus stacked on the floor. I was allowed to borrow as many as I liked but she was very strict about the treatment and return of the books. "Don't turn back the pages to keep your place." She gave me a book mark. "And don't write in the margins. If you find something you want to remember, buy a little notebook and write it down."
I've still got the bookmark and I am on my fiftieth notebook.
I read *Huckleberry Finn, Tom Sawyer, Treasure Island, Robinson Crusoe, The Thirty Nine Steps, Swallows and Amazons, Gulliver's Travels,* Enid Blyton, all the classics of childhood including Louisa M Walcott and Richmael Crompton.
My love of history was increased by reading Walter Scott's Waverley novels. Later came Edgar Wallace, *Biggles* and CS Forester. At Blessing's urging I read

Wordsworth and Byron, Anne of Green Gables and all the *"What Katy Did Next"* books.

Blessing was an amazingly fast reader and was well on the way to devouring the whole of her mother's collection. Shelia had shields and medals displayed on her mantelpiece for hockey and tennis. She had represented Surrey at tennis and still played at the local club with the other lady who lived in the house, Edith.

"Our lodger" said Blessing. Edith and Sheila had met at Wimbledon.

Sheila had been a line judge and Edith in charge of the ladies dressing room for the Wimbledon Fortnight. The rest of the year she worked in the Wimbledon office as an accountant. She knew all the players, the famous ones as well as the younger ones on their way up or down. A writer called Nancy Spain was a big friend and I came to know her later on. Edith was a woman with strong arms and hands and a broad bottom, a bit older I think than Sheila. Her hair was cut short. She told me that was how she had worn it in the army. Edith came from Yorkshire and loved to exaggerate her accent to make us laugh. "I won't take me coat off, I'm not stopping."

After a couple of large sweet sherries she would sing *On Ilkley Moor Bar Tat*.

She was in her spare time a Girl Guide Commissioner and sat on lots of committees. When not out on her official visits she spent much of her time in the garden.

I watched her as she dug and planted and she would reel off the names of the flowers in Latin, puffing on a Woodbine cigarette. The household had a calm and pleasant atmosphere, only disturbed by the yapping of Edith's Jack Russell, Toby.

Edith had a wind-up gramophone and a collection of Louis Armstrong and Django Reinhardt, Frank Sinatra and the Ink Spots records.

There was also a Pianola. These were pianos with a pneumatic mechanism that operated the piano action through pre-programmed music perforated paper.

You put a roll of perforated paper in the slot above the keys and set it going.

Out would pour Mozart, Beethoven and old music hall numbers, the keys moving without any human contact or musical skill. They had been going out of favour but a revival in interest kept them going throughout the sixties.

Blessing and I gave masterful concerts with one or the other of us conducting to a grand finale when the roof would come off with the wild applause from Sheila and Edith. They reserved the biggest cheers for *"Knees Up Mother Brown"* especially when we substituted the second line with "Your drawers are hanging down."

Sheila and Edith had a tandem bicycle on which they went for rides into the countryside at weekends or around Greenwich Park.

Blessing was a very pretty girl, taller than me, lithe and quick in manner and movement. Her eyes were a dark brown and always seemed to be on fire.

She would come over to my house and we pored over sports annuals, comics, biographies. My mother would sometimes let her stay the night, especially on "Big Fight" nights. We hugged the wireless close to our ears in the kitchen in our pyjamas, dressing gowns and slippers, with a cup of cocoa and Peek Frean custard cream biscuits clutched in our hands. Bruce Woodcock fought before 50,000 people at White City and lost the Heavy Weight Championship or Freddie Mills was battered into submission by an American Middle weight. The commentator of boxing matches on BBC Radio was a fruity-voiced man called Raymond Glendenning.

At the end of each round he would say "Come in Barrington Dalby."

Barrington would give a whisky-soaked opinion on the progress of the fight, never forgetting to mention that "The British Boy was fighting with great courage and had a great chance against the American visitor."

Usually Woodcock was knocked out in the next round.

Blessing went to the same primary school as me.

Going to school through Greenwich Park, I was the Czech runner Emil Zatopek winning three Olympic gold medals, the most amazing one being the marathon because I had never run one before.

Blessing was the Dutch sprinter Fanny Blankers Koen, a simple housewife, her hair pinned back in a seemly bun as she won four gold medals at the 1948 Olympics.

Our training runs were dedicated to both of them, before the moment of truth arrived.

There was an awesome moment as we left for school and lined up and waited for the starting gun, our feet firmly in the starting blocks.

We had the odd false start so we had to retreat to the first beech tree before placing our hands down again, getting our feet comfortably into the blocks again, and peering towards the prize of the finishing line and the tape.

"Do you know what I am proudest of Ricky?" Blessing said after she breasted the tape for her first gold medal just outside the school gates.

"No" I panted, just having won the 3,000 metres in record time.

"This" and she shyly took from her Maths book a piece of paper with the picture and signature of Jesse Owens, a four medalled winner at the Berlin Olympics.

"I got this in Berlin in 1936."
"Jesse Owens; *the Jesse Owens?*"
"Yes. I went up to him and said I'm Fanny Blankers-Koen.
He said "Pleased to meet you young lady, I'm Jesse Owens."
"He shook my hand. I was trembling with nervousness.
He had these lovely gentle brown eyes.
Hitler hated him"
"Why?"
"Because he was… well you know like me"
"What do you mean?"
"In case you haven't noticed, I'm black Ricky."
"More brown," I said.
Blessing cuffed me round the head.
"Oh come on let's go."

Jesse Owens

"The only bond worth anything between human beings is their humanness."

Blessing's remark set me to consulting my sports books. It led to a serious commitment from both of us to become two black American athletes, Jesse Owens and Wilma Randolph.

I had to become a track and field star at Ohio State University so I went into serious training in the Park and garden. I stopped eating Garibaldis for a week, and did press-ups on the lawn and stand-ups on the iron staircase leading into the garden from the study. Breathing exercises and short sharp sprints under my trainer's supervision started to make a big difference. I won the first of my eight individual NCCA Championships. Interviewed by a reporter from the local newspaper, I was suitably modest though not happy with his calling me "boy" and his patronising manner. Despite the acclaim I was beginning to receive I had to live within America's vicious racist society. At Blessing's house I had to sit at a separate table waited on by Blessing doing her Baby Doll/Carol Baker accent.

"Y'all want sunny-side up eggs and muffins with your cawfee honey child?"

Sheila and Edith ignored us. That was until I asked if I could stay the night. Both of them looked shocked.

"No negroes sleeping in this house boy" said Edith.

I did lots of part time jobs to work my way through college.

We put aside a whole day for the 1936 Berlin Olympics and booked Edith to play Hitler. She cleared the garden tools away and made a podium out of some garden seats and wooden boards. The irony in coming from racist America to the land of fascism and anti- semites was that I had no trouble booking into the same hotels as whites in Berlin without either hotel proprietors, Frau Edith and Frau Sheila batting an eyelid. Edith did a wonderful Hitler impression, borrowing from the cinema news reels and Charlie Chaplin in the Great Dictator.

The atmosphere at The Olympic Stadium was awe inspiring and for a short moment I felt intimidated. One of my German opponents pointed out Hitler and Goebbels in a box but their names meant nothing to me. I felt like most Americans, that the world beyond America was a peculiar place of weird and insane people. They were the foreigners, not us. I leapt a record distance into the sand in the long jump.

I scorched around the track in the 100 and 200 hundred metres with my coach Blessing screaming her head off. I finally ran a leg of the winning relay.

I had made history with four gold medals. Hitler jumped from the podium and goose stepped into the kitchen to make tea but he waved to me and I returned the wave.

The German people were kind to me and came up to me in the streets to ask for an autograph. On my return to America I was given a ticker tape parade.

Edith, Sheila and Blessing threw wedding confetti over me as I waved regally from an open topped wheel barrow.

"That must have been a sensational experience" said the interviewer.

"Well, yes but to get into the reception honouring my achievement they wouldn't let me ride the hotel elevator at the Waldorf Astoria, so I had to take the freight elevator.

The papers were full of the story that Hitler had snubbed me but he didn't. Roosevelt did. That man was a racist, frightened of losing the Southern vote.

I never got a telegram or was invited to the White House."

"Things got tough for you later on. At one time you raced against horses."

"What was I supposed to do? I had four gold medals. You can't eat four gold medals."

"Why did you smoke?"

"Yeh thirty five years I smoked. Maybe I was stupid."

"You died from lung cancer."

"It figures.

"I died in 1980 aged sixty six. I had been one of eleven children. My Grandaddy was a slave, my daddy a share cropper. We left the segregated South in the Great Migration with more than a million others. I foolishly thought there would be no segregation in Ohio. I have been more honoured since I died than in my lifetime. The one that makes me smile the most is the street named after me in Berlin near the Olympic Stadium. Jesse Owen Allee.

Wilma told me I had been her inspiration."

Wilma Rudolph

"I spent most of my time trying to figure out how to get my braces off."

Sheila and Edith made splints for Wilma's twisted legs caused by Infantile Paralysis as a very young child.

"My parents took it in turns to take me to the hospital for treatment.

I was one of twenty two children. My Mammy and Daddy were upright God-fearing Americans but they was also black and living in Tennessee.

Life was tough for anyone in that part of America but tougher if you were black.

But our house was full of love. At times I despaired of getting better but I prayed to the Lord. One day the doctor called me into his consulting room and told me I would never walk again. I came out crying and told my mother.

My mother was a very tough and positive lady."

"Honey, you will walk again."

"Maybe I won't Mammy."

"Who do you believe Wilma, the doctor or your mother?"

I looked at her. Hope and belief were etched into her shining face.

"I believe you Mammy."

Wilma's appetite was a thing of wonder as she trained ferociously. Crisps, tinned peaches, tinned John West salmon chunks, sherbet dabs and sticks of liquorice, plates of green cabbage and roast potatoes. Heaped plates of porridge with the cream off the top of the milk and a spoonful of Tate and Lyle Treacle fuelled her training runs before school. The broken biscuit box was always empty.

"Thanks to my parents and the physiotherapist at the hospital I recovered. It felt like a miracle and I built up my strength. I started playing basketball and loved it.

I became a bit of a star but one day I was spotted as a possible track runner.

Running released something in my body and my soul. On the track I was in a zone. It became a drug and my obsession. I saw film of Jesse Owens and thought of his fantastic achievements. At night I dreamt of Olympic glory.

"The 1960 Olympics," I said in hushed tones.

"That was my year, you betcha."

Wilma crouched down. The raucous crowd went silent. Edith fired the gun and Wilma tore round the course, winning the one hundred metres without running out of breath. In the two hundred she had to strain a little to reach the tape first. The four times one hundred metres were her third Gold Medal, as the crowd went wild and she was in the history books.

"The Italians called me "La Gazella Negre, The Black Gazelle,"

The French,

"La Perle Noire, The Black Pearl."

I went home and did a degree and became an elementary school teacher. Later I commented for television on sports events.

I've got a life sized statue handcrafted from bronze on Cumberland River Walk and the Wilma Randolph Boulevard in Clarkesville, Tennessee.

Not bad for a girl from a poor family and starting life as a cripple."

Wilma contracted brain and throat cancer and died at the early age of fifty four.

She was a soul sister to my friend Wilson who I will tell more of later.

She said, "I loved the feeling of freedom in running, the fresh air, the feeling that the only person I'm competing with is me."

1953 – The Coronation

"I, Phillip Duke of Edinburgh, do become your liege man of life and limb and of earthly worship and faith and truth will I bear unto you to live and die, against all manner of folks, So help me God."

1953 was the Coronation of Queen Elisabeth II.

My mother, my sister Susan, Sheila, Edith, Blessing and myself went up on the bus the night before and grabbed a pitch on the edge of Parliament Square.

My mother had packed the awful cheap "pacamacs," plastic raincoats that gave off an unpleasant odour. We were glad she had because, of course, it rained during the evening. We had thermos flasks of cocoa and tea, Smith's Crisp packets with a twist of salt at the bottom, cheese and yellow pickle on white bread sandwiches and my mother's famous rock cakes, so hard I could use them as cricket balls; which Blessing and I proceeded to do, using a rolled up umbrella as a bat.

I bowled and Blessing struck rock cake after rock cake into a laughing crowd.

My mother led the crowd in song as the rain teemed down and then led an impromptu Conga around the square. The news came through during the night that Edmund Hilary and Sherpa Tensing had conquered Everest. *Land of Hope and Glory* rang out and three cheers were called for.

We were a bedraggled crowd the next morning that roared for the Queen's coach and even louder for the Queen of Tonga, an ebullient and beaming large lady waving regally from her gold coach. No-one knew where Tonga was but it didn't matter. Sleepy but thrilled by the events, I felt a great warmth for my country and laughed at the banter on the bus back home. It is not always a proud history I celebrate, being all too aware of the horrors we have perpetrated as a nation. But at its best we can surprise ourselves with a sense of honour and an ability to recognise our hypocrisies and laugh at ourselves.

1953
The Magnificent Magyars
Goodbye to all that.

The year 1953 was seminal in English football. The English team, before a crowd of 105,000 at Wembley, were stunned by Hungary with a display of total football, beating us 6-3, inflicting our first ever defeat on home soil for ninety years and then rubbing it in with a 7-1 victory in Budapest. I was a school boy sentenced to my usual ignominious place outside the room for bad behaviour but even the Geography teacher passing by told me the score, both of us aghast at the seismic news.

Hungary introduced us to the concept of a deep lying centre forward who could score goals. Nandor Hidekuti was that man, scoring three times.

Ferenc Puskas showed us how to roll a ball back and forward, scoring a sublime goal.

Sandor Koscis was the supreme goal scorer and playmaker, Josef Bozsik was an attacking wing half. Billy Wright, the icon of the English side was bewitched, bothered and bewildered by the fast and criss crossing patterns of the Hungarian's passes.

I have a souvenir programme of the return in Budapest with wonderful photographs of the goals scored and the crowd's reactions. The caption to a picture of two men with earphones says,

"An innovation of the Hungarian radio: After each score a former outstanding footballer gives a quick analysis from behind the goal for the listeners."

Wilson the Wonder Athlete

"I just run, and somehow if I forget I'm racing and only jog-trot along until I don't know I'm running, I always win the race."
The Loneliness of the Long Distance Runner.

The seminal moment in my sporting, intellectual and spiritual life came when I met Wilson. Wilson the Wonder Athlete had a grip on my affections and later became a close friend, guide and mentor. He was in late middle age when we met, always dressed in black. He first came to my attention when he emerged from a crowd waiting for a race to start in Charlton Park and joined the lined up runners. The crowd were mystified. Who was he? He ran a three minute mile according to my watch and before he disappeared back into the crowd, I ran after him and managed to talk to him.

He had piercing blue eyes and not an ounce of surplus flesh on his tanned body. Wilson was over six feet tall; his black hair was long at the back and tied into a pony tail, unusual in those days and evidently self cut. He didn't walk so much as glide along. Every sentence he spoke was carefully pondered, weighed and succinctly delivered. Any show of affection came only through his eyes.

Admonitions travelled the same route and were like an examination of your insides.

I poured out my heart to him telling him of my desire to achieve world domination in the steeplechase. I'd seen Christopher Brasher on a grainy Pathe News at the local cinema winning the 3,000 steeplechase in 1956 in Melbourne so I toyed for a while with becoming him.

Wilson listened carefully and promised me I could go and see him one day if I promised secrecy. He lived in a cave in Yorkshire, eating mainly berries and nuts. Wilson had travelled the world, studied medicine and biology and worked out a fitness regime for longevity as an athlete and passed on some of his lore to me.

He never sought publicity or glory and went on to win marathons, hurdles, steeplechases. He told me under oath that he had been given the gift of eternal life by a hermit from Ilkley Moor. Wilson lived in a cave whose location has never been revealed and I am not going to break the promise I made to him all those years ago.

Like the graceful and quiet man that he was, he will glide in and out of these pages at his own pace.

He had a small circle of friends and later introduced me to Roy of the Rovers, star of Melchester Rovers, a diminutive cultivated goal scoring centre forward. Roy had a greased quiff, spoke with a Northern accent, and loved the music hall.

He and Wilson did a double act, taking off the comedienne Hylda Baker.

Her catch phrase was "Well I'll go to the foot of our stairs."
She had a music hall routine in which she, a very little lady, had a very tall partner. The tall one would nod in acquiescence at everything Hylda said.
Hylda would crane her neck to look up at her partner and say to the audience in a knowing way, "She knows, you know."

It is impossible to say why it was so funny because it was all in the facial and physical movements, betraying her training in music hall tradition denied to comedians today.

Sadly Roy lost a foot in a helicopter crash and became a not very successful manager unlike Blessing who was already managing Tottenham Hotspur.

Radio Times

I grew up listening to the radio and my mother took me to Lewisham Hippodrome to see Michael Bentine, Frankie Howerd, Ted Ray and others.

Tommy Cooper was a great favourite of Blessing and mine. Flo, my mother took us to see him at the London Palladium. The stage was dark as we sat waiting.

Then we started to hear the unmistakeable voice of Tommy. He was banging about, bumping into furniture saying "ooh" "ouch" and so on.

Finally he said "where's the lights?."

At last he stood before us, the audience already roaring with laughter.

He had a violin in one hand and a painting in the other.

"I went up into the attic the other day, found these.

I took them to an antique expert… well, you would, wouldn't you?

Or you might not. I don't know, do I?

The man said "Mr Cooper; you have a Stradivarius and a Rembrandt. Unfortunately…, Stradivarius couldn't paint and Rembrandt couldn't play the violin."

Cooper then thrust the violin through the painting.

Blessing and I listened to all the comedy shows on the wireless.

ITMA with Tommy Handley, *Raise a Laugh* with Ted Ray, *Take It From Here* with the great June Whitfield who is still going strong at 86.

The sad genius, Tony Hancock, and the ebullient Sid James in *Hancock's Half Hour*, *Round the Horne* had Kenneth Williams with his high-camp and multi accents.

One of the most successful shows strangely, was *Educating Archie*.

Archie was a wooden dummy voiced very badly on the stage by the ventriloquist Peter Brough whose lips could be seen moving all the time.

The radio show was a contradiction of the art of the ventriloquist but was loved by all.

Sundays were Roast beef and potatoes, Yorkshire pudding, overcooked vegetables, all covered in congealed thick brown gravy. The musical background was *The Billy Cotton Band Show* and later on, *Family Favourites, Life with The Lyons, Meet the Huggets.*

Our weekday treat was *Dick Barton Special Agent,* with Snowy and Jock.

Finally all our generation were ensnared in the anarchic world of the *Goon Show* graced by the ebullient Harry Secombe, Spike Milligan, Michael Bentine and the paranoiac genius Peter Sellers.

They've Kicked Out Baldy Hogan

"Football is about glory;
it is about going out and doing things in style and with a flourish."
Danny Blanchflower.

Another friend of Wilson and a man who had a big influence on my football career was Baldy Hogan, an avuncular and honest man. I played for his team Burhill United. Baldy was player manager and did everything. He marked out the lines, put up the nets, rubbed Vaseline on sore heels. Put cotton wool in our boots and got the oranges at half time. On cold days he put a drop of rum in our tea cups. Baldy was puzzled by our goalkeeper's lapses. The keeper would make some amazing saves and then suddenly let in an easy goal. After being driven home by him and going through several red traffic lights, Baldy worked out the goalkeeper was colour blind and started to put name tags on players socks and on the goalposts and corner flags.

I can see Baldy now, his Cup and League medals swinging from his watch chain, his bald pate glistening with sweat as he put a bladder in the leather case and pumped up the ball, lacing it within seconds. He played out on the left wing and I pushed balls inside the right back for Baldy to run onto and lash into the net. "Just lay it on my left foot Ricky and bosh, it's all over. You see, you're the artist who sees the whole canvas, the visionary painter. I'm the executioner." The ungrateful owners of the club eventually sacked him for poor results when Baldy the guillotine master started to fail to whack the ball home with much consistency. The local paper ran the headline,

"They've Kicked Out Baldy Hogan."

My early career before that included playing for a Youth Club in Deptford where blokes aged twenty five or more indulged my trickery and ruffled my hair when I scored. The goal keeper was censorious Reggie Tutt, or Tut Tut as we called him.

A rotund father of four children he was also a demon table tennis player of the defensive variety, standing well back and returning every ball with a chopping motion that drove me to distraction. I was persuaded to move on when a friend I played with on the local housing estate nicknamed "Kidda" Johnson who in his mind was really the deep lying Hungarian centre forward Hidegkuti, asked me to join Young Christian Workers. We were neither Christians in any real sense or workers but we were young. Our managers were the Virgo brothers, nicknamed the Virgins.

They wouldn't hear of Blessing playing for us despite my pleadings.

She was better than most of them but... a girl? No Way! Get back to dolls and dresses.

Hidegkuti was more in Kidda's mind than his feet. A tall but frail figure, by the time he had thought out what to do with the ball, he had been crunched to death by the opposing deep lying centre half. The league we played in was a weak one and I scored dozens of goals. I had to contend with the animosity and jealousy of Terry Tierney who had been their star until I arrived. He wasn't a bad player but terribly slow and pedestrian, expecting the ball to arrive for him to put away without too much strain on his dodgy knees. He said that once I'd got hold of the ball, he could go to the cinema, come back an hour later and I still wouldn't have released the ball.

I have to admit he had a point.

I was attracting attention from other local clubs and was sitting on the bus on my way to Woolwich for a Tony Curtis haircut at Luigi's Barber Shop and to buy a seventy eight gramophone record of *I Believe* by Frankie Lane.

Reggie Brooks, the local hard man feared by us all sat opposite.

Brooksie was a legend. He once had held off three neanderthals at a dance hall in Eltham, hammering them into the ground. For good measure he belted a policeman, incurring an extra misdemeanour. He was "bound over to keep the peace" an unlikely scenario for a volatile young man.

This led to further legendary stories where unable to fight personally he stood on a chair pointing out those to be whacked by his gang.

It was rumoured he was spoilt by his Mum and Dad who were rather proud of his reputation and called him Reginald. He wasn't very tall but carried an air of brooding menace, a sort of Brando like stare. He played for UGB Pantiles, the best local team, as a left winger. He had dark curly hair and was wearing a duffel coat, the coat we all yearned to own.

"You're Ricky Morris right?"

"Er... yeh."

"We're expecting you for training on Tuesday night."

You didn't mess with Brooksie. I nodded and duly went along to the ground.

United Glass Bottles was a major Charlton firm. To play for the youth team, one was supposed to have a relative working there, but the rule was ignored by Geordie Harrison the manager. Within a few weeks I was playing at White Hart Lane in a youth cup final. The captain of our team was a fresh faced right half, modest and unassuming and a fine passer of the ball. Barry became my closest male friend and still is, fifty five years on. He had lost his father from a direct hit on the house in Woolwich they shared with other family members in 1940.

Barry is universally loved by all who know him. My daughters adore him. He is considered as part of the family by the Frenchies, my sister Susan's family.

Many people in Woolwich worked for the giant German and English firm, Siemens.

The unusually long shelter at the tram stop protected the workers from rain and snow. Barry's grandmother had converted the front room of the house into a haberdashery shop. Her biggest sellers were seamed nylons and she gave tick (credit) to the girls from Siemens.

Barry and I shared a sense of humour, a sense of fairness, sympathy for the underdog and a love of sport. Still do.

Tennis Dreams

*"A perfect combination of violent action taking place
in an atmosphere of total tranquillity."*
Billie Jean King.

In a hot summer of that year I took up tennis, training and playing against the back wall of our new home in Vanbrugh Park, Blackheath and was soon beating all the best players; Emmo, Kramer, Sedgeman, Kenny Rosewall and my friend Drobny.

Jaroslav Drobny was one of those special characters sport gives birth to.

He was a Czech. Poor Czechoslovakia had been born as a nation in 1919, lost its independence under the Nazis, briefly regained it after the war, only to be destroyed again by the virus of the Soviet Republic. Drob had been a silver medallist ice hockey player for his country in the 1948 Olympics.

A vicious slash from a opponent's blade had given him eye trouble and he wore thick glasses for the rest of his life. He lived in Tooting, London and we met in a local park in Durnsford Road where this charming man sat with his dog watching me play.

He came over and said in his thick accent,

"Come I vill show you how to hit a backhand." Afterwards he bought us ice cream and talked of Czechoslovakia. He was a well educated man and introduced me to Eastern European history and its culture. Prague, he said was in the middle of Europe and for centuries had been an important hub for the exchange of ideas and artistic endeavour amongst many nationalities.

He told me to read Kafka and Kundera.

Drob gave me lots of tennis lessons and invited me to Wimbledon to watch him play Jack Kramer in the last sixteen of the tournament. Wimbledon was strictly amateur then and so full of ghastly snobs as to make the air reek of hypocrisy.

I sat on Centre Court as Drob beat the favourite Jack Kramer.

He then lost in the semi-final.

Drob had had enough of the surreal and Orwellian life under Communism he led in his country and fled, travelling on an Egyptian passport.

In 1951 Barry and I took our first trip to Paris to watch him play in the French Open. Sheila and Blessing had been before, but were just as excited as us.

We went on a boat from Newhaven to Dieppe being disgustingly sick for the whole of the three and a half hour journey, our faces literally turning green.

We loved Paris with its wide boulevards, customers sitting on the pavement outside cafes reading newspapers, the indifferent waiters dressed like penguins, people greeting each other with handshakes and kisses on the cheeks. The girls were chic and stunning, with legs that went on for ever, the sun shone and Barry and I decided we must learn French if only to chat to the ladies .

It was a shock to see red clay instead of grass at Roland Garros and to hear the partisan crowds baying for their local favourites. Drob won the title and went back and won it again the following year. The best was yet to come for my friend.

He lost in two Wimbledon finals but aged thirty two beat the diminutive and hugely talented youngster Kenny Rosewall to become the Champion. He was the first lefthander to win the Wimbledon title since the Australian Norman Brookes in 1914.

I kept in touch with him and his lovely wife Rita over the years and often visited his sports shop in London. He finally became a British citizen in 1959 and died aged eighty in 2001 after suffering a series of strokes.

I played a lot of tennis with Blessing or Margaret Court as she became.

Court was the only player to win all twelve Grand Slam titles. Twice!

She had a booming serve, a relentless pressure approach and sometimes some dodgy calls or at least that's what I claimed when she beat me, which was most of the time.

If we had known that Miss Court was to go on to become a bigot with a perverted view of her fellow humans, I doubt Blessing would have chosen her as someone to aspire to.

She founded a Pentecostal Church and made a speech in Parliament House in Canberra.

"Homosexuality is an abomination to the Lord!

Abortion is an abomination to the Lord!"

Her special insight into the workings of the Almighty made her oppose laws that gave equal rights to gays. Why on earth would the Australian government then decide in 2007 to make her *An Officer of The Order of Australia?*

It was apparently for her services to tennis and as a mentor to the community.

The sporting gods produce special athletes to lighten and enhance our lives.

Lew Hoad was handsome, blond and muscled whom everybody loved except perhaps Pancho Gonzales, another legend with a volatile temperament. I was introduced to Lew and Kramer by Drob and was immediately in awe of Lew's talent and personality. I took the opportunity offered by Jack Kramer to travel around with the players in London when Jack began the professional era by signing up the top players to play each other all over the world. Due to all my commitments I could only be in London, with my hero.

I used to carry Lew's bag for him. He was blond haired and muscular with sparkling blue eyes. I sat entranced as I realised what sort of a player and man he was.

Life was to be lived; "get in there, do your thing and get out mate" was his credo. Long serious conversations like long tennis rallies were not in his repertoire or vocabulary. Pulp fiction was his reading matter. On court he was like a boxer going for the quick knockout, always trying to hit winners from whatever shot he received and wherever he was on the court. Sublimely confident in his abilities he rarely lost in his early years. He was a prodigious drinker. Before he won the French Open he told me he downed three bottles of white wine and some beers the night before.

I sympathised with his back problems, an affliction which I shared.

He retired to run a tennis school in Spain and was friends with the rich and famous. Sadly leukaemia and a heart attack killed him at fifty nine years of age.

He's up there with the tennis gods.

Rest in peace Lew.

Cricketing Times

"Cricket lovely Cricket it was at Lords where I saw it with those little pals of mine Ramadhin and Valentine."

Blessing and I took a bus to Lords for the famous second Test in 1950.

Sheila had prepared cheese and marmite sandwiches, a bottle of Tizer, a packet of crisps and an apple each, all placed in an old tin box with Jacobs Cream Crackers, Extra Light written on the top.

It was the first time we had been to a Cricket ground and we were struck by the colours. Pennants fluttering in the breeze like the miniature sails of a yacht; the grass so green it stung the eyes as the white painted stands blinded us too. We stood like two little sailor cadets stranded on a foreign shore, unable to speak or move.

An avuncular old man in a blazer and red tie ushered us along, helped us find our seats and we sat down slowly as if afraid to disturb the upturned seat.

We knew little of the ritual and protocol of a day at Lords.

A kindly man with sparkling eyes and wearing a Panama hat sitting next to us became our friend and guide for the day. We understood why a bell rang; we applauded the Umpires as they made their pedestrian way to the middle. We only stretched our legs when drinks were being taken or in between wickets. We clapped fours, well run singles, cheered for sixes. Catches and wickets too, of course, but especially thunderous clapping when the stumps were scattered and the bails flew yards away.

We went into reveries as the fast bowler took for ever to walk back to his mark and thrilled us as he tore into the wicket and released a blur of red too fast for our eyes to follow. We found out what a no-ball was. During the lunch break we were introduced to the art of the googly by our friend who just happened to have a tennis ball in his pocket. Arthur bought us an ice cream each. It was a day of initiation into a world that I have never left. The West Indian spinners took 19 wickets between them. Cyril Washbrook scored a century but Clyde Walcott scored 168.

It was the first time a West Indian team had beaten England in England but we were neutrals that day. The joy on the faces of the relatively few West Indian spectators was intoxicating and infectious and the Lord's crowd was generous and sporting in its reactions.

We said "thank you" and "good bye" to Arthur and our other new friends sitting the other side. We sat on the top deck of the bus and didn't stop talking on the way home and planned our first Test Match together in the garden.

Blessing was going to be Clyde Walcott. "No arguments Ricky" so I settled for Ramadhin. Blessing's mother sat smiling benignly as we regaled her with our day, pouring out our tale in a torrent of almost incoherent language.

I slept in a cocoon of delicious dreams, reliving every shot, every ball bowled and saw myself striding to the wicket like Clyde Walcott.

Cycling Mania

"Cycling is like a church. Many attend but few understand."
Eddie Merck 5 times winner of The Tour De France.

Cricket and football took a back seat for a while when Blessing became Beryl Burton and I became Reg Harris. Neither of us had ever taken much interest in the tandem in the hall. We thought it a strange intrusion amongst the tennis rackets.

One day Sheila and Edith took us to meet the man who had made the bicycle, Claud Butler. He had a workshop in Clapham called the Manor Street Works. We arrived to find a jazz band playing, a Punch and Judy show and acrobats on mini bikes doing all sorts of tricks. Claud was a bushy browed man, stick thin and slightly bent over. Edith said it was because wherever he was or whatever he was doing, in his mind he was on a bike hanging over the handle bars racing to the finishing line.

His bicycles were works of art in a bronze weld construction with fancy lugs and a light frame. Sheila explained that Claud had these festivities from time to time to promote his bikes. Edith greeted a very fit looking lady and introduced her as Beryl Burton; "A very famous cyclist, Blessing and Ricky. I used to race against her at our club in Morley." Beryl seemed an intense and highly-strung character.

Edith grinned. "She never beat me, kids" she said, "and this is her husband Charlie."

A rather shy man shook our hands.

Beryl slapped him on the back. "My best mate and best mechanic since the day we met. Always there for me, aren't you love?" she said.

"It was his shoes that attracted me. I was crossing the floor at the tailoring firm where we both worked. I suddenly heard the clicking of cycling shoes.

I looked down; they were right gorgeous with metal cleats on the side which made the clicking sound. I thought he must be alright then.

I never looked at his face. Only joking Charlie love."

Blessing was looking at Beryl's bike. "Like it do you love?"

She grabbed a bike from Claud's stock.

"See if you can keep up with me." The two of them raced off.

A balding stocky man came over and grinned at us.

"She's never off duty" is she?

Do you want a race young man?"

I confidently raced off on the bike provided, never guessing I was racing the cycling legend, Reg Harris. Blessing came back after me. Reg had sprinted well but I guessed he was going slower than his normal pace so as not to embarrass me. He lit a *Craven A* and puffed away, blowing smoke rings to my delight, as he told me about his triumphs.

"You see Ricky; every sport has its rituals and techniques. Start yourself off slowly and build up to pace. You need to find a rhythm but your own rhythm.

Don't tense up but relax into the ride.

Shut out any other thoughts except finishing first. If someone passes you don't chase madly after them but keep to your pace and gradually build up your speed.

On your training runs keep telling yourself you are an athlete and cycling is an extension of acrobatics."

Blessing came round the corner, trailing Beryl. Her eyes were shining and I knew in her mind she was already on the podium as Beryl Burton, Champion.

We went home on the bus, our legs metaphorically pumping the pedals, our backs bent over the handlebars, our eyes on the finishing tape.

Our first bikes were Raleigh Lentons, the Reg Harris Sports Road Model which had been remodelled in 1955. It had curved handlebars, mudguards, thin tapering back stays. The lamp bracket was switched from stem to right hand fork and it had hooded brake levers.

Reg's signature was on the seat tube and it cost £19 and ten pence.

Blessing had insisted on having a man's bike too. She had a job in the local library and I was still doing my paper round and delivering beer in the evenings.

Our first serious run after racing around Greenwich Park was to Southend.

We decided it would be a time trial. Reg was known as a sprinter and Beryl as a distance cyclist but we ignored that distinction. We set off through Tower Hamlets at six in the morning. It was 59 miles to Southend. It was raining when we started, rained all the day and all the way home. We ploughed along country lanes with mud flying up into our eyes and rain dripping down our collars and down our backs. The posters advertising Southend on Sea on railway stations boasted of seven miles of glorious seafront and the longest Pier in the world.

Well, we found our way through the mist to the Pier and gazed mournfully out to where we believed the sea to be.

Our hearts weren't really into laughing at our distorted features in the Hall of Mirrors.

We did venture onto the beach but the wind and driving rain drove us back onto the promenade. Beryl was the first to snap out of our dreary spirits. We set off home and gradually got into a rhythm as Reg and Beryl. I seemed to have the edge on Beryl.

My breathing was good, my legs responded to the extra push I demanded from them. I looked back from time to time to see Beryl apparently struggling but she waved cheerfully and urged me on. As we approached home, I was dreaming of a mug of Bovril, slices of bread and dripping and a hot bath. Suddenly Beryl raced past me and shouted over her shoulder.

"Want a liquorice allsorts love?"

I was not amused but I felt ready to become Reg.

After poring over war books from Sheila's collection, I served in the Tenth Hussars in North Africa driving a tank, before being wounded and invalided out.

I was determined to win gold at the 1948 Olympics. A few weeks before the event I fractured two vertebrae in a road accident, then fractured my elbow in a fall from my bike in training. I had a spirit of steel and turned up at the Olympics with my elbow in plaster. I don't want to make excuses but I only managed two silvers. When I turned professional I won the British title four times. Like so many sportsman I hated "civvy" life. I still cycled every day and spent most of my life in cycling gear even when walking the dog.

Life was tough for the ladies in my life. The threat "It's me or the bike" was never going to be a contest. I spent the winter of 1973 training every day and came out of retirement in 1974 aged fifty four to win the British Sprint Title. I never read books or went to the cinema, never fished or gardened. When I wasn't on a bike I felt diminished and not quite secure or together. Even going to bed, in my mind I was on a bike cycling upstairs. I just pray there are bikes and race tracks in Heaven."

Reg collapsed when cycling near his home.

He was buried in St John's Church in Cheshire.

His memorial is in the Manchester Velodrome, cast in bronze with a plinth of Welsh slate, a depiction of a hump backed sprinter curving round the bend, his eyes on the finish. Beryl revered Reg. But she said she always resented the publicity Reg got which she as a woman didn't.

"I had a phenomenal career. Seven world titles, silvers, bronze. I used to beat all the men. When I overtook Mike McNamara in the twelve hour time trial I offered him a liquorice allsorts. I did 277.25 miles in the time limit. I regret my rivalry with my daughter. I never really understood how that happened. Maybe I was too wrapped up in my own career but when she out sprinted me in 1975 I felt humiliated.

Refusing to shake hands with her was something I always regretted."

Beryl Burton never really reconciled herself to retirement. A few weeks before she died she was entered for the national 10 mile championship.

She was awarded an MBE and an OBE. The Beryl Burton Cycle Way allows cyclists to travel two point eight kilometres between Harrogate and Knaresborough without using the A59.

Blessing and I never stopped cycling but decided we wanted to pursue other sports as a full-time career.

Part Two

Parting

"Parting is such sweet sorrow."

Sheila said she had some news but it could wait until tomorrow.
The bad news was that Blessing's father wanted her to go to Jamaica to live with him for a while. Blessing's mother, unusually for a grown-up, told me to call her by her first name. The three of us talked about it and what sort of country Jamaica might be. "Very hot, lively music, political tensions and some wonderful cricketers as you now know." Blessing's father was a Methodist Preacher. He and Sheila had met at his church in Brixton. They were married briefly before he met someone else at a Methodist Conference and went back to Jamaica. Blessing had six step brothers and sisters she had never met.
Sheila was so calm. "I think it would be a great experience for you."
"What about you Mum?"
"I'll be fine and I am sure Ricky and Edith will keep an eye on me."
"Oh Mum, I'll always love you"
"Of course you will and I'll always love you.
It isn't for ever, for ever. Take the chance and go."
I had to endure further shocks before she left.
One day when we were alone in the house, we took off our clothes and solemnly examined each other's bodies. Blessing had the beginnings of breasts and seemed much bolder than me, manipulating my penis into an erection. We experimented with various positions, Blessing told me what was supposed to happen but it was all text book stuff she'd read and as she solemnly explained the technicalities it led to a loss of libido and we ended up abandoning the action. We sat morosely at different ends of the sofa drinking Tizer and nibbling custard and cream biscuits, tacitly agreeing to end that part of our relationship. We never spoke of that day again.

I had the freedom to go into the house at any time.

During the summer holidays I went over to call for Blessing and went in through the back door. It was very quiet and I gazed out of the window. In the shade of the apple tree, Sheila and Edith were kissing passionately and clinging to each other.

Sheila turned and saw me. I fled. It was a shock but I didn't really understand what it meant. Two women together seemed strange to me. What had made it seem incongruous was that Edith was in her Commissioner's Uniform with her hat on but wearing her gardening boots. Sheila was wearing her nightgown with a tiara of daises.

The next day Sheila asked if she could talk to me on my own.

Quietly she explained to me that love between women wasn't evil any more than love between two men was. "We have different ways of releasing our sexual energies but they all amount to the same thing. I should know; I've tried both."

I asked her if Blessing knew and she nodded her head.

"Promise you will talk to her about it."

We sat in the garden and Blessing said, "I didn't know the word Lesbian or dyke until Mum explained the words, just like Queen Victoria who refused to believe in their existence. Samuel Goldwyn, the Hollywood producer when told a film couldn't be made because it featured two Lesbians, replied

"No problem, let's make them Albanians." I suddenly got the joke and the giggles.

We clung together helpless with laughter.

It was a still warm day and I loved Blessing more than ever.

If anything I became closer to Sheila. She always hugged me when I went into the house. Edith slapped me on the back and ruffled my hair;

"Alright Maestro?"

At Tilbury Docks I had my heart broken for the second time. I was fine on the trip down in Sheila's Wolsey. Okay in the waiting area, engrossed by the comings and goings of staff, people and jaunty shouting sailors. Luggage was thrown around, cargo stacked, horns blown. Seagulls made a horrendous din and I could smell the sea.

The final call came over the loudspeaker.

Sheila and Blessing hugged, with Blessing clinging to her mother. Blessing then rushed off without a word or even a look at me. As she started to go up the gang plank, she turned and shouted, "Tottenham Hotspur for ever."

I stood transfixed and the tears started to roll as I realised what I was losing.

Not just Fanny Blankers Koen but Margaret Court, Clyde Walcott, Wilma Rudolph, Roger Bannister, Beryl Burton, Billy Steel, Raich Carter, Len Shackleton, Jackie Stamp, Charlie Vaughan; a mighty host, an army of sportsmen, a team, a galaxy of sporting giants. Who would replace Eddie Bailey, Ted Ditchburn, Billy Nicholson, and Danny Blanchflower?

Who would be the manager of Tottenham?

I was inconsolable on the way home.

Sheila as ever cheered me up by saying Blessing would soon be back and maybe I should take over as Tottenham's manager.

But of course those glorious times were gone, never to be brought back except in the shades and cloisters of our memories. Life does, we know, move on.

Great moments were yet to come for both of us.

Sally

Dogs lives are too short. Their only fault really.

The first time my heart had been broken was when Sally died.

Sally was a Battersea Dogs Home refugee rescued by Flo, my mother.

She had a sandy coloured coat, big lustrous eyes and a perpetual wagging tail, she was attached to me like an umbilical cord. Sally slept on my bed and followed me every waking hour. If I sat down she sat down. If I got up it had to be the opportunity for walkies. She loved playing football and was a demon dribbler. A tennis ball tossed high in the air was caught expertly in the mouth. She knew all my worries and moods and took them on her shoulders, listening intently and cocking her ears, or snuggling up to me on the bed. After twelve years Sally started to fade. I tried to ignore her decline but when she disappeared into the bushes in the garden and lay silent, her eyes unseeing but her tail still wagging when I spoke, I had to face the inevitable.

I thought of her as Odysseus's dog Argos. After twenty years Odysseus returned from his heroic voyages and found Argos lying on a pile of manure covered in lice, old and tired. Argos recognised Odysseus but had only the strength to wag her tail, turn over and die. I carried Sally to the vet in my arms and thought of her final resting place in a dog's Valhalla. I didn't even cry on the way home, just loved her and mourned her.

Still do.

Football Again

"People always remember the second half."
Graham Taylor.

In the football season of 1960-1 *"Those glory glory days"* Danny Blanchflower, the erudite captain and right half of Tottenham Hotspur led them to the Double, winning The League and FA Cup. They played like Barcelona and the Spanish national team play today. Short passing routines set up a rhythm which opposing teams found difficult to break up. Dave Mackay was a frightening prospect bearing down on a hapless forward. They had a solid defence of goalkeeper Bill Brown, full backs Peter Baker, Ron Henry and centre half Maurice Norman.

Cliff Jones was a very fast winger fearless in running at the opposition as was Terry Dyson and Terry Medwin all of whom were supplied with sublime passing by John White and Les Allen. Bobby Smith, the rotund centre forward brooked no sledging or harsh tackles and gave like for like. John White died cruelly at age 27 when struck by lightning on a golf course whilst sheltering from a storm

I don't need fantasy football or cricket games on a screen, filtered through unimaginative minds or screaming commentators, they're all there in technicolour in my imagination,

I've been living the beautiful game all my life in my mind.

I wrote for the magazine of the Young Christian Workers at age 15 the following in **1954**

Young Christian Workers FC
Semper fidelis
Fourth Edition August 1954

The World Cup has just been staged in Switzerland. From this event England have learned, finally, that instead of being the leading football nation, we are now hardly ranked in the first four. Why has this state been reached in English football?

I think it is not because of sundry excuses about the climate and bad luck etc, but

because the English refuse to learn from others,

We were beaten 6-3 by the Hungarians at Wembley, our first home defeat ever. What happens?

In the return match at Budapest no change whatsoever. The England team is picked a few days before the match, sent to Budapest and humiliatingly beaten 7-1.

Again what happens?

The World Cup players are first picked and then dropped. The greatest player of all time, the Maestro Matthews is omitted and then finally picked.

Infamy that there should ever have been any doubt.

They prepare for the first game by playing a game of rounders!

Compare this to Uruguay who had before their match with England a 90 minute non-stop passing session. The secret of the Continental success seems to be their willingness to learn, their amazing ball control and the use of the open space.

I contend that England, given the chance could play our old type of football that footballers of the Carter, Mannion, James era played and thrash the continentals.

It will be another four years before there is another World Cup. In that time, England can build a team to take that cup from the Germans.

Richard. J. Morris – Inside Forward

In the FA Cup Final in 1953, then one of most popular competitions in the country, Stanley Matthews inspired Blackpool to come back from 3-1 down to win 4-3, Stanley Mortensen scoring a hat-trick. I first met Stanley Matthews at Charlton when I was a ground staff boy. He came out to have a look at the Valley pitch before the game. We chatted briefly and he told me not to smoke or drink if I wanted a long career. On the pitch he and Ernie Taylor did a lovely trick I have never forgotten.

Stanley would dribble up the wing, dance about a bit and then suddenly run past the full back leaving the ball behind and the full back chasing him. Ernie would whip quickly in and take the ball over. Years later in Glasgow, Stanley was standing at the desk of the hotel where I was staying and I went up to him and said

"You're Stanley Matthews."

"I know son, who are you?"

He remembered me and introduced me to his companion.

"This is Bill Perry. He scored the winning goal in the Matthews Final."

They both grinned. Bill Perry had left South Africa as young man where if he had remained he would have been classified as Coloured under apartheid laws.

He had thirteen successful years at Blackpool. His goal had come in injury time from the left wing. I knew Mortenson had said, "I left it for Bill" but Perry said it was out of Morty's reach and he had just let fly and crunched the ball home.

We had a long chat about our careers and mutual friends including of course Sam Bartram. I reminded Stan of the Ernie Taylor trick and he smiled wistfully.

He was intrigued to hear I was a friend of Wilson and asked if he could meet him.

"I still feel I could play some useful stuff for a club."

Stanley had played until he was fifty and must have been over seventy when I met him in Scotland. At the end of our chat, he said "See what you can do about meeting Wilson." I never did manage to arrange the meeting.

We shook hands. "Thanks Ricky for taking the trouble to come and talk to me."

I choked back the tears hearing this idol of mine acting so humbly.

I think the truly great are like that. No ego, no side, a genuine interest in the fans and other aspects of life.

Keith Miller, a great friend of Denis Compton was in the same mould, an extraordinary human being, a true maverick.

Keith Miller

When once he was asked about the pressures of Test match cricket, he replied "Pressure is a Messerschmitt up your arse, cricket is not."

I met Keith by chance. I was on the Tube once going to Lords when at the St John's Wood exit I found myself walking alongside him and introduced myself.

We talked as if we were old friends.

"Call me Nugget." he said, his nickname after the press had called him a golden boy.

I didn't dare to at first. He was the cricket correspondent for The Daily Express and various Australian news outlets. As our friendship blossomed I soon accepted that a different woman would be on his arm each time we met for drinks or meals in London pubs. Excursions to the phone booth for him were only to find out if his horse or dog had romped home in that day's races. Win or lose we caroused the night away.

Keith was one of the greatest all rounder's ever, though restricted by back trouble.

He was a brave pilot in World War II and was deeply affected by the carnage and horror of war. He was once fined for using insulting language to a superior officer. We discovered that we both loved opera, over a bottle of wine one evening.

I had a friend Bill who worked at Covent Garden Opera House as Chief Electrician. He was a big cricket fan. I arranged to bring Keith in for a tour backstage. The area surrounding Covent Garden was still a fruit and vegetable market then and Keith was assailed from all side by workers and owners of stalls, not all the shouts being complimentary.

He of course loved it and gave it back with spades.

He strode through the market like the Prince he was. Hair flowing, shoulders swinging, leaning slightly forward like a boxer on his toes. Though I knew it was because his back was sore.

The scene shifters and back stage staff were absolutely chuffed to see the great man and no-one was refused a handshake or an autograph. Praise the gods that camera phones were not around then. The instant proof of proximity to the famous or mildly well known craved by the modern world was not yet invading every private and public moment.

The backstage area is huge and we were both fascinated by the machinery and amount of people involved in a production.

We went out onto the front of the stage to be confronted by Geraint Evans the great Welsh baritone, waiting for a rehearsal to end. I had once sold him a rocking chair in my antique shop days and he gave me a slap on the back," Hasn't broken yet, still rocking" he said.

A Singing legend and a Cricket legend stared at each other with admiration. Geraint said,

"You should see my cover drive and my late cut.

I also bowl useful off spin.

I always wanted to walk out at Lords and score a century Keith."

Keith said,

"You should hear my Don Giovanni, brings the house down"

Bill wickedly said "Keith has always wanted to sing at Covent Garden, Geraint."

"Well go on then Boyo." Do your worst."

Miller bravely struck a pose, put a hand on his chest and sang a few bars from Don Giovanni.

"La ci darem la mano."

"Ever thought of becoming a soprano Keith?" was Geraint's response.

We toddled off to the pub for several hours where both men regaled us with stories from cricket and opera and I went to bed that night with a sore head. Old age treated Keith cruelly, reduced to a wheel chair and intensive care.

Alice Marble

"When the day comes that a woman who is athletic will no longer be regarded as the unusual type, we'll start training girls to be active athletes."

It wasn't until I met another legend, Doug Wright that I developed my devastating leg breaks. Blessing had come back into my life. Sheila and her father had agreed to send her to a girls school in Kent. Sheila had always kept me in the picture on her life in Jamaica and I had seen photographs of her with her father. Sheila told me Blessing was playing a lot of cricket but her obsession was with running.

"Blessing's back." Sheila's phone call was a thrill and I rushed over to see Blessing. The reality when we met again was breathtaking. She had shot up to over six feet, had biceps that made mine look puny and bounced around on the balls of her feet as if preparing to strike an opponent. Her hair style was Afro, her skin gleaming and she looked like an African Princess. As ever words poured out of her in an endless torrent of comment on every sport in the world, every book ever written. She had been the youngest female to represent Jamaica in cricket matches against Australia and England taking seven wickets in one innings and scoring a century in another. In the Commonwealth Games, still a teenager she had won a bronze in the Heptathlon and came fourth in the Long Jump.

I of course knew all the facts from Sheila who never failed to read out Blessing's letters home to me but as she told me of her sporting life, I realised she was a serious athlete. She was hyper and Sheila and Edith couldn't stop laughing at her enthusiasm. We all went to Charlton Park and smashed tennis balls all over the place on the grass court. She played well but the canny Sheila conserved her energy, lobbed and spun with Edith hanging her nose over the net and putting away every weak return.

They hammered us.

"What happened to Margaret Court?"
"What happened to Lew Hoad?" Blessing countered.
Sheila and Edith were very excited about something but wouldn't say what. Finally after persistent questioning Edith said
"Staying with us this weekend is Alice Marble."
We looked dumbfounded, having no idea who Alice Marble was.
"She was one of the greatest tennis players ever."

Nothing could have prepared us for Alice Marble. Blond and vivacious with legs that went on forever, her eyes sparkled with wicked humour.

We were in love with her from the moment she put her arms around us and said,

"I've heard a lot about you two stars and we're going to have a lot of fun."

And we did until her death in 1990. Alice was truly a life force and captivated men and women alike. Edith told us about Alice's relationship with her coach Teach Tennant who according to Edith had been in love with Alice for most of her life. Teach had persevered with Alice from her chubby teenage years through to her Wimbledon win in 1939. But at that first meeting we talked about all the stars she knew and had played tennis and partied with. She not only knew Charlie Chaplin but Bing Crosby, David Niven, Marlene Dietrich, Errol Flynn, Douglas Fairbanks and Mary Pickford, the list was endless. She had been a member of the gilded circle at Hearst Castle in California, visited today by thousands of tourists but in her time a fiefdom of the newspaper owner on whom Orson Welles based his character *Citizen Kane*. It wasn't Alice's style to tell vain stories of her days with the stars but rather to tell scandalous tales about them and do very funny impersonations of some of them.

Her great friend had been Carole Lombard and she had adored Clark Gable.

That didn't stop her from telling the story of the premiere of *Gone With the Wind*, the hugely successful American Civil War film. Gable, a private and shy man took a bath in the hotel where they were all staying. Lombard called Alice and said,

"You have to see this."

Apparently the word had gone out from the hotel staff and from Lombard's room they could see people in the hotels across the road with binoculars straining from every window to catch a glimpse of the great man in the nude.

After much giggling Alice asked Carole if she shouldn't go and warn Gable to draw the blinds.

"What and spoil their fun. Let them look. Besides if they see his manly weapon they'll find it's a dinky little thing."

Alice had overcome serious illness and injuries to forge her career at the top of the women's game. She had also overcome the trauma of being raped as a teenager in Golden Gate Park, San Francisco. When she came to London she would take me and Blessing to musicals, museums, restaurants, buy us clothes, and lavish hugs, kisses and love on us. Over the years we knew Alice, she gradually revealed stories that were hard to believe. She had sung in night clubs and even been in a Hollywood movie. Teach was the tennis technical advisor on the movie *Pat and Mike* starring Spencer Tracy and Katherine Hepburn. She recruited Alice and other stars like Donald Budge and set up sequences with the camera showing one side of the net at a time.

Budge would hit, Alice would volley with the camera on Hepburn.

One day she casually dropped into the conversation that she had been a spy for the American government in the Second World War. We were incredulous and the thought that she was making it up showed in our reaction.
It sparked her into action.

"I was trained to kill."

She went through a simulated rapid fire movement of taking a weapon from under her arm.

"I could pull the clip and reload in seconds. The secret service trained me to hit man sized cardboard silhouettes. Stand up Ricky. Now come at me with arms raised."

Before I knew it Alice had thrown me on my back and sat astride me pinning my arms to the ground. Of course she had to do the same to Blessing and Blessing of course had to be better than me in resisting. Alice prevailed and forced a plea from Blessing,

"to go easy."

Alice, absolutely fired up, then said,

"Believe me now you little punks?"

It was only after she died that her book *Courting Danger* told the full story and it reads like a Hitchcock movie. She had been flown to Switzerland ostensibly to play exhibition matches but the Intelligence Services wanted her to link up with a former boyfriend. Hans was a rich Swiss banker who had all the top Nazi's bank accounts and their gold in the cellar of his castle home. Her job was to photograph the evidence.

The Americans were determined that the Nazis wouldn't be able to flee with all their tainted money. Naturally Alice and the Swiss fell in love all over again.

She managed to get into the cellar but was disturbed by the staff and Hans and fled in his car. Chased by several cars, she pulled over in relief when she saw the face of her Intelligence contact. He was a double agent and shot her as she, realising this, tried to flee. Rescued by American Intelligence officers she was holed up in a private clinic to recover from her wounds, sworn to secrecy and then returned to a normal life.

Yes, I still don't believe it but...

For me her finest hour had been when she wrote an editorial in support of Althea Gibson in 1950 to American Lawn Tennis Magazine.

Althea and Angela

"Minorities Win."

"No matter what accomplishment you make, somebody helped you." – **Althea Gibson**
"I think the anti-Semitism is still there." – **Angela Buxton**

The endemic racism of American society runs through every facet of its daily life.

Gibson had been refused entry to the American Open because she was black.

This was five years after the war when thousands of Black Americans had given their lives for America and its "freedoms."

Further the Armed forces were segregated throughout World War II.

Alice wrote "Miss Gibson is over a very cunningly wrought barrel and I can only hope to loosen a few of its staves with one lone opinion. If tennis is a game for ladies and gentlemen, it's also time we acted a little more like gentle people and less like sanctimonious hypocrites, If Althea Gibson represents a challenge to the present crop of women playing it is only fair that they should meet that challenge on the courts. If they do not I would be bitterly ashamed."

Britain's hands are tainted with the same stains against common humanity. Angela Buxton, a feisty player from Northern England was being coached as a young player at The Cumberland Club in Hampstead. When she applied for membership she was told she had no chance because she was Jewish. She also suffered the same humiliation in Los Angeles. The British and Americans had a vicious strain of anti-Semitism running through its society and golf and tennis clubs harboured nasty WASP members in the United States.

In Britain the ghastly antics of the Mitford sisters, Unity and Diana with their fawning and drooling behaviour with Hitler and his ilk and the effete and racist Duke of Windsor were just at the top of an undistinguished pile of garbage mentalities in Britain.

I worked for a time at Lillywhites, the sports store in Piccadilly. I was a shoe salesman and from time to time had to climb the stairs to the fourth floor to fetch new stock. Behind a huge pile of shoe boxes sat a handsome blond lady taking shorthand from the shoe manager. Miss Buxton never deigned to acknowledge my lowly presence. One day there was a tall black lady waiting for the down lift.

She gave me a big grin. "Hi young fella, how's it going?" She stuck out her hand.

"I'm Althea Gibson and I'm going to win Wimbledon soon.

I've been to see my friend Angela. Do you know her?"

"You're American."

"Sure am "boy." I'm from Harlem."

She had said the magic word. I had read a lot about the Harlem Renaissance and its subsequent history. In my imagination I had been there. I had listened to Fats Waller, Jelly Roll Morton and Willie "The Lion" Smith. I'd been "Stomping at the Savoy."

I'd drunk cocktails at The Apollo whist listening to Billie Holiday, Ella and the "Divine" Sara. I'd read Richard Wright and James Baldwin.

I poured all this out to Althea in a rapid torrent of excitement.

She stood there grinning and interjecting "wows" and "hey's."

"Come on, I'll take you for tea and cake."

I didn't hesitate and thought to hell with the job if my manager is angry when I get back. I never did go back except to get sacked and my employment papers.

We went to a café nearby. Althea told me she had recorded at the Apollo Theatre, another miraculous connection. Her life had been hard, growing up poor in Harlem. But she had always played sport of some kind. She had defeated all comers at Paddle ball, a game played with a wooden paddle and a rubber ball on the streets of Harlem.

As she grew older she took up tennis but as ever had to deal with American racism.

On one trip to play in a black only tournament she told me that when the bus reached Bluefields, Virginia, the driver halted the bus, stepped from his seat, faced the passengers. "We are about to enter the State of Virginia. By law all coloured persons must move to the back of the bus."

Because of Althea's great talent she began the process of integration.

She told me a wonderful Groucho Marx story. Jews were generally banned from "white" golf clubs. One club told Groucho he could join if he didn't use the swimming pool. Groucho replied "My daughter is only half Jewish. Can she wade in up to her knees?" The wonderful sequel to all her struggles is that she met and bonded with Angela on a tennis tour of India. They went on to win the French and Wimbledon doubles titles together. Angela reached the Wimbledon final where she lost to Shirley Fry but won on the same day the Wimbledon Doubles with Althea. "Minorities win" was one national newspaper's headline.

Althea won Wimbledon twice and The US Open.

She and Buxton stayed in touch over the years. Buxton came to Gibson's rescue when in later life Althea fell on hard times. She had two cerebral aneurysms and a stroke. The hospital bills destroyed her savings. In desperation she wrote to Buxton asking for help. Angela wrote an article in a tennis magazine outlining Althea's plight.

Over a million dollars came in from all over the world.

Buxton herself became a very successful business woman running sports and tennis centres.

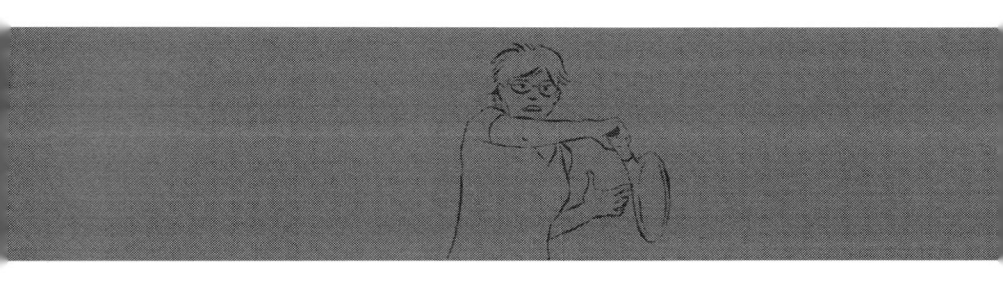

Billie Jean King

*"The main thing is to care.
Care very hard, even if it is only a game you are playing."*

Alice followed all the new players with avid interest. Her involvement led to her coaching of Billie Jean King. She was around when Billie rose to the challenge of Bobby Riggs. Alice and Bobby had won their Wimbledon titles the same year of 1939.

She was fond of him but knew what a chancer he was. He would bet on anything but especially on himself.

Bobby had challenged Margaret Court to a match and after beating her, said,

"I want Billie Jean King, the women's lib leader; I'm going to teach her that men are superior in every facet of life."

Alice paid for us to go to Houston for the game.

Billie told us. "Tennis has always been reserved for the rich, the white, and the males. Since I was a little girl I have pledged myself to do everything in my power to change that."

Billie introduced us to one of the greatest ever women's doubles players, Rosie Casals. Rosie had been ranked number three in singles at one time but had never won a Grand Slam. In doubles with Billie she won 112 titles on every surface, winning Wimbledon and the American Open in 1967. She was tiny and ferocious in conversation, as she was in playing tennis.

"Listen you two English gin and tonic socialists you don't even begin to understand the tough life. In America if you're gay and from an ethnic minority you start off with a weight on your back. It weighs even more if you are poor. My parents couldn't afford us, me and my sister, and farmed us out to my mother's sister and uncles and aunts."

Blessing burst out, "But that's why you became a champion, not only at tennis but for women's lib. You are famous, rich and you give a lot back into the world."

Rosie looked fierce but couldn't resist Blessing's earnest face;

"Okay sweetheart, I know I whinge too much about the past but, what's the phrase?"

"The price of peace is eternal vigilance"

"Well, in American society Blessing Baby, the price of dignity is eternal lobbying and protecting yourself from the bigots. Americans have never faced up to the two great social crimes that haunt American history and continue to sour and bedevil relationships today; the removal of the Indians and the enslavement of the Africans.

There is a vicious undercurrent of racism and hatred towards African Americans, gay people and women who want control of their own bodies."

The pre-match insults mounted up. Bobby Riggs was interviewed wearing a skirt.

"This is men's Liberation. If I'm going to be a male chauvinist pig I'm going to be number one." Rosie countered with "He's an old man (he was fifty five, Billie was thirty), who walks like a duck, can't see, can't hear and besides, he's an idiot."

The day of the match the weather was as ever in Houston hot and sultry.

Thirty thousand spectators were packed into the auditorium eating burnt meat, sucking ice lollies and quaffing coke and sodas. We were entertained by bands and cheer leaders.

Fanfares announced the arrival of Riggs as he entered the Houston Drome in a gilded carriage pulled by scantily dressed women.

Billie Jean came in on a red velvet litter carried by University of Houston football players. Bille had told us that this match was as important to her as any of the titles she had won. She demolished Riggs 6-4 6-3 6-3.

Riggs was noble in defeat. "She was too good, too fast, returned all my passing shots and made great play off them." Gracious in victory, Bille said she hoped the match would help a lot of people to realise that, "everyone can have a skill whether you are a man or a woman as well as help men and women to understand each other."

Riggs and King stayed friends until his death from prostate cancer in 1995. Rosie Casals said "For a male chauvinist he did a lot of good for us.

We'll always remember him in the best possible way."

Part Three

> *"Well if your baby leaves you*
> *You got a tale to tell*
> *Just take a walk down Lonely Street*
> *To Heartbreak Hotel."*
> Elvis Presley

Musical Chairs

My young years were borne along by a background of music.

The 1950's were Guy Mitchell, Tennessee Ernie Ford, Frankie Lane, Johnny Ray and Jo Stafford.

My mother had an old wind-up gramophone and some ancient 78's with people like Frank Sinatra singing, "*Begin the Beguine.*" Then came the craze of skiffle groups, Elvis, Buddy Holly, The Blues and Jazz. In one glorious year I saw Satchmo, Count Basie, Duke Ellington, Ella Fitzgerald and Nat King Cole in concert.

Saturday nights were spent at The Hot Club of Woolwich with Chris Barber, Ken Colyer and Kenny Ball. My introduction to opera was the film with an all-black cast, *Carmen Jones,* starring the stunning Dorothy Dandridge and handsome Harry Belafonte.

I jived, crept, and bopped and was a peripheral figure, hiding behind the back row seats at the first rock and roll riot at the Woolwich Odeon where Bill Haley and the Comets drove the crowd wild with *Rocking Round The Clock.*

I also began to be aware of the class-ridden society I was growing up in. Being on the cusp of working class and middle class attitudes could have left me confused. I was fortunate that somehow I never believed in that nonsense and refused to accept my mother's subservience to the idea of superiority by virtue of birth or wealth. If I attempted to use the vocabulary I was imbibing from Sheila and the books I was reading, my mother and other members of the family would come out with phrases like "have you swallowed a dictionary?". People with money and a big house were deferred to. Doctors and Solicitors with appalling manners were deferred to. Some people went home to have their tea at six o'clock, others to have their dinner at seven. On the few black and white television screens I saw at friend's houses, the strangulated vowels of Malcolm Muggeridge and his ilk ruled the medium and caused much mirth and imitation amongst us.

The prejudice of southerners against northerners was stifled when realistic drama and sex came along. Working-class actors started to rule the world.

Albert Finney in *Saturday Night Sunday Morning*, Tom Courtenay in *The Loneliness of The Long Distance Runner* and *Billy Liar* with the stunning Julie Christie, a brooding, simmering Richard Harris in *This Sporting Life*.
was a tour de force of directing and acting.

John Braine wrote *Room at the Top* starring Laurence Harvey, the charismatic Donald Wolfit and the incredible Simone Signoret and then sank into sodden decline.

I never bought into that game of "So what school did you go to?
Or "What does your Father do?"

Even dear old Denis Compton succumbed. I saw him once at Blackheath Tennis Club playing in a Cricket charity game sucking up to some dreary and useless old Lord Foot and Mouth. "Yes my Lord, of course I can play in your charity game."

The England of that period was still mired in racism, dreams of Empire and class prejudices. Maybe it still is for some. But not me. Wherever my journey would take me it would not be down a racist road, or forelock touching foolishness

My friends and I had innate good manners. We stood up and opened doors for women. We gave our seats up on the tube and trains to older people, to pregnant ladies. No-one told us to do it. We just grew up surrounded by adults who behaved like that and followed their example.

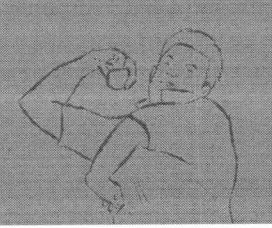

The Ashes and Doug Wright

The Art of Spin

"When you're an off spinner there's not a lot of point glaring at a batsman. If I glared at Viv Richards he'd just hit me even further."
David Acfield. Off Spinner for Essex.

Blessing went to her new school in the spring and immediately got into the cricket team. Jane Wright became a friend and Blessing discovered she was the daughter of Doug Wright, a captain of Kent and England Cricketer.

Both of us were invited to tea one day in their house in Kent. Tea in china cups, paper doilys, and cucumber and cress sandwiches cut into little wedges.

Doug Wright was a shy man with a self deprecating air and smile.

He always wore his jacket in the house and smoked a pipe.

Somnolent dogs lay at his feet, a purring cat on his lap.

We chatted for ages and Doug was obviously taken with Blessing as most people were on meeting her. She made him laugh when she suggested he should bring a team to play the girls at St Margaret's.

However, a seed had been planted in his mind. Doug had a word with the Kent Committee and it was agreed that history would be made, a benefit match, the first time a County Cricket team had ever played against a girl's school.

The publicity was huge with reporters from Australia, New Zealand, South Africa, Pakistan and Ceylon descending on St Margaret's on May 3 1957.

ITV filmed the event and showed it that evening. The game attracted over a thousand spectators. Doug presented all the girls with miniature bats autographed by the Kent County Team. Much as she loved the occasion, Blessing was miffed that the County players deliberately dropped catches and generally fooled around.

I had been studying the art of leg spin bowling in my spare time and had serious talks with Doug on the subject. He had played thirty four Test matches for England and his selection was always surrounded by controversy. He had a run-up as long as a pace bowler though he leapt in long strides rather than ran in. His potent whipping leg breaks and googlies depended on dry pitches and he could be very expensive.

Doug loved to talk about the techniques of leg spin. He emphasised to me that only right handed players could be leggies using the wrist rather than the finger spin of off spinners. However he demonstrated how a left arm delivery from a spin bowler could produce a leg break spinning from left to right. This delivery was called a Chinaman. I began to dream of this delivery. What if I developed an orthodox right arm leg spin but supplemented it with a left arm Chinaman from time to time to disturb the batsmen? Dougie had endless patience showing me how to get my grip just right.

He understood all aspects of spin and what I was trying to do.

He taught me how to drop the ball into the rough or get into the block hole without being belted for four. Doug never worried about being whacked for consecutive fours.

He bided his time and struck like a cobra.

It was some years after meeting him that I returned to the game when Michael Brearley persuaded me out of retirement for an Ashes series.

I was persuaded to play in the 1981 Ashes series when Mike Brearley became captain again after Botham's disastrous sojourn. I'd got to know Mike when a close friend of mine was going though a bad patch in her life. After searching for help, I came across Mike and I arranged for her to see him. He was a psychoanalyst and psychotherapist, a profound thinker but essentially down to earth and enormously kind.

We struck up a friendship and found we both loved the theatre, poetry and history.

He was a principled man who had opposed links with apartheid South Africa in 1968, supporting John Arlott's campaign in The Guardian.

I loved the later story that after being elected President of MCC, Mike took a bus home.

He had seen me play for Surrey Seconds a few times but I was not a leading cricketer by any means. However when I did play I took lots of wickets and tales of my leg breaks were causing interest. We had dinner together and got very excited about Indian philosophy and Gerald Manley Hopkins' poetry.

We also got very excited about a St Emilion, so excited we decided on a third bottle with the cheese. Mike started drawing an ideal field for leg spinners on the table cloth.

He said he saw me as an ally for intelligent and fair cricket and maybe a surprise packet for the Aussies with my leg spin. I took a deep breath, another piece of cheese and glass of wine, promised to do some training and I was hooked.

The series didn't really come alive until the Headingly Test. I had contributed very little except as ever, my legendary close catching. I was soaked in the atmosphere and loving the proximity of so many talented players. Brearley's genius was to release Botham from any sour thoughts about losing the captaincy or fear his form was deserting him for ever. Beefy was too right wing for me. He positively adored Margaret Thatcher. It seemed strange for such a large hearted and generous person.

It always struck me that under all the bravado and bluster he was intellectually insecure, in awe of the cerebral Brearley, as indeed the Australians were.

Botham was a fearsome sight in his cups, a bottle of brandy and red wine the night before a game was no problem for his constitution. It just increased his volubility and exacerbated even more his silly opinions on politics, the Royal Family or socialism.

There was very little intelligent or thought out argument in his addled brain. The game was to all intents over when we left Australia with only 130 to win.

I had bowled well for short periods but my back was having violent spasms, striking me constantly. Mike as ever quickly grasped the situation and hid me at gulley where I snapped up two catches.

When we were batting in the second innings, Botham went into a zone of his own.

His brute strength, his eye and hand co-ordination, his sheer bravado was a beautiful thing to witness. Not a blink of an eye, not a step back. He scored 149 not out supported magnificently by Dilley and Willis. It was rousing and exciting for the crowd but the real drama, the play within the play was yet to come.

When we bowled, I realised I would have no part to play except fielding to the best my creaky back would allow. Mike and I had a look at the pitch and could see cracks and fissures that would respond to any balls short of a length. Before lunch Bob Willis was cranky, offline and bowling far too many no balls. As we walked out after lunch Mike was in deep conversation with Bob.

"Don't worry about your field, don't worry about bowling no balls, and don't worry about anything except bowling the fastest you have ever bowled. Leave the rest to me."

I have never seen anybody so focussed. It was Zen like. Bob was fired up but in control. His eyes flashed with anger but controlled anger. His run-up was like a prancing race horse, a Derby winner coming in sideways on and carving a furrow in the pitch. Over the years so many people think of that game as Botham's, but it was Bob who won it and should have taken the laurels of victory.

Eight for 43 are good figures by any standard but in the situation they were stupendous. Modestly I rarely mention my catching in that match but people still come up to me in the street to rave over my contribution. For one catch I made at least ten feet to snatch the ball inches from the turf. For another I fell backwards clutching a smashed cover drive that threatened to break my fingers.

The one everyone remembers is when I turned and chased after a lofted drive everyone except me had given up on and sprawling with my nose to the turf, I caught it just inside the ropes. The crowd erupted and at tea I was given a standing ovation, even the hyped up Bob Willis hugging me to his chest. Mike just grinned and shook my hand. He had never scored loads of runs for England but his captaincy was unique. He had the antennae of an animal in the wild listening for danger. He knew when the slip cordon was losing concentration, who was bored in the field, who was muttering about not getting a bowl. His field adjustments were a series of nuances, slight but crucial.

Mike could crack the whip or placate an angry and frustrated player. Above all he had the respect of the team, they sensed that he knew exactly what he was doing and it instilled confidence in all around him. The big egos fought back but took his advice. Mike told Botham that he was using a far too heavy bat. That was like challenging the biggest bull in the bull ring. Botham hurled a mouthful of abuse at him. When he went out to bat he was carrying a lighter bat. His bowling heroics at Edgbaston in the Fourth Test when he took five for one were a result of Brearley brooking no argument in ordering Botham to replace his trainers with proper bowling boots. Boycott was told that he was standing too far outside the crease and playing across the line. The arrogant yet insecure Boycott asked Brearley

"Ow many Test runs have you got then?" When he arrived at the middle all of us could see he was further back in the crease and playing with a very straight bat.

He got a century but still didn't have the grace to acknowledge that Mike had been right. Brearley was also instrumental in changing a law of the game. In 1979 in Australia Brearley had faced down the childish tantrums of Dennis Lillie.

Lillie had come out to bat with an aluminium bat which was perfectly legal at the time. However the bat appeared to be damaging the ball and Brearley complained to the umpires. A ten minute conference took place until Greg Chappell the Australian captain instructed Lillie to use a wooden bat. The fiery Dennis threw the aluminium bat over forty yards towards the pavilion.

Later it transpired that Lillie had used the bat for a publicity stunt. The bat was being marketed as a replacement for expensive wooden bats in schools and developing countries, with Lillie taking a cut. Sales of the bat were phenomenal after the incident. The tolerant and good humoured Brearley signed the bat after the match;

"Good luck with the sales." However the authorities amended the laws of the game shortly afterwards stating that all bats must be made of wood.

I sat down with Mike after the game and told him I thought my time was up. To have continuous success as a leg spinner, I needed dry pitches and wasn't getting too many of them. My back condition meant that bowling the Chinaman was taking too much toll and causing me too much pain.

I knew that for me this particular party was over.

I thanked Mike and took the train back to London.

There is something civilised about cricket that appeals to my sensibilities.

It's rare or at least used to be, to get boorish behaviour from the players.

I was around when the never ending line of West Indian fast bowlers and supreme batsmen were instrumental in the West Indies becoming a World cricket power.

The advent of brutal fast bowling from Roberts, Garner, Holding, and Marshall et al. was to bring in helmets, intimidation and death threatening bouncers.

"Whispering Death" was Holding's nickname. Number elevens lost their immunity from bouncers. Did something go out of the game? Chivalry?

The arrogant swagger of Viv Richards, the lashing of the ball to the boundary by Clive Lloyd as if trying to destroy the ball, the intensity of the fielders, the delight taken in striking the batsmen.

But a little delving into the history of colonialism makes one understand what that was all about.

C.L.R James

"What do they know of cricket, who only cricket know?"
Beyond A Boundary

I was fortunate to meet C.L.R. James in a library in Brixton where I had gone to do some research into colonialism. I had been reading Orientalism by Edward Said and articles he had written. His admiration of James was profound.

I had read *The Black Jacobins* but also what is considered the masterpiece of cricket writing, *Beyond A Boundary*.

I had just sat down when I saw this old man looking at me.

I nodded and then a tremor passed through my body. It was him. C.L.R. James.

He was quite frail but his six foot frame and long legs made him tower over me. A deep and resonant speaking voice reminded me of his eloquence over the years. His history is an amazing saga of dedication to West Indian emancipation, humanism and racial harmony. I walked over and asked if I could buy him a coffee.

"You can do better than that. You look affluent. Buy me lunch."

Several hours and two bottles of wine later, I realised why the lines in *Beyond A Boundary* were so well known. The hinterland of so many people in the public eye is restricted to the job in hand and they do not reach out for the treasury of knowledge so close at hand, an act which would widen their sympathies and sensitivities.

I got for the price of lunch, a seminar on West Indies history and the effect that the British occupation of the Caribbean and dominance of its people had upon his generation. I also got his view that Sobers was the greatest all rounder ever, that Botham was the only Englishman who would have made the West Indian team.

He loved Rohan Kanhai. "The greatest batsmen break the rules. Rohan did this falling hook shot, finishing his follow through lying on his back. When he played for Ashington in 1964 the crowd adored him. I think he's the only cricketer to have a pub named after him." CLR had been a noted lady killer and his views on women and their roles in life were a century or so out of date. James was the first Black Caribbean to have a book published in the United Kingdom. He led the campaign for a black cricket captain of the West Indies team which led to Frank Worrel's appointment. James had grown up in a society dominated by cricket.

The Trinidad League had clubs divided by class, race and skin colour.

Despite his lifelong identification with the West Indian struggle for independence and the colonial nature of British society, he was an intellectual who wrote for the Manchester Guardian and a play starring Paul Robeson.

He saw that the importance of the game in the West Indies was instrumental in forming a national culture and the eventual decolonization of the Caribbean. A recent London Film Festival showed a marvelous documentary, called *Fire over Babylon* which in thrilling close-up demonstrates that the West Indies were no longer to be taken lightly and intimidated by the likes of Thomson and Lillee.

The aggression was payback time for the arrogance of the Australians and English over some humiliating years.

Tony Greig in an interview before the Test matches said,

"We are going to make them grovel." The West Indies carried out two blackwashes of the hapless English team. Richards was supreme, batting without a helmet. England players are shown in the film being bombarded by bouncers with the foolhardy Brian Close being continually hit. When the commentators and press complained, the West Indians reminded them of Larwood and body line in Australia. C.L.R. said

"I learnt that the values of fair play and acceptance without complaint inculcated in me by my English type public school education rarely applied in the political sphere."

I never met C.L.R. James again but his enthusiasm burns so brightly in my memory that I think of him with a quill pen in one hand and a cricket ball in the other, chatting to anyone who would listen about literature and cricket.

What would he have made of the insouciant Chris Gayle, a recent West Indies captain saying, "It wouldn't be so bad if Test Cricket died and was quietly buried?"

Another sportsman seduced by the money in the game of sport, in this case The Indian Cricket League which is sustained by crooked gambling syndicates and rich men's money.

I may be wrong but it is hard to think of many football writers with C.L.R's kind of background and breadth of knowledge, though there are many fine writers on the game. In the past Brian Glanville and Geoffrey Green were supreme in the field.

Football writers must find it difficult with most footballers and their supporters' anti-intellectualism, limited communication skills, short attention spans and boring after training routines for the players. Night clubs are their natural habitat; books are not to be read but to be on shelves, not in your kit bag. Hours are taken up with discussions with agents, fashion advisers, architects, all dedicated to filling their lives and making money, instead of practising their skills and broadening their horizons.

220,000 a week, a five book deal for your jejune life story and Rooney's too tired at 24 years of age to perform for his country in a World Cup!

What can we expect when these boys in perennial short pants wearing gold pendants around their necks and wrist watches as large as Big Ben finish their education around nine or ten and can't string a sentence together?

Frank Lampard went to a private school but I am yet to discern an ability to express himself on any subject with wit or humour, or an awareness of what irony is.

We're hardly likely to have a player called Socrates in our country.

Samba football doesn't have to produce samba minds.

Socrates

"Man was born into trouble as the sparks fly upward."

Socrates Brasiero Sampaio de Souza Viera studied to become a Doctor whilst still playing. I met him when I became involved with a friend of the owner and manager of Garforth Town of the Northern Counties East Football League. Simon Clifford ran Socatots, coaching schools with strong links to Brazil. Garforth is a former mining town, but is now a commuter link for Leeds and has a very boring Town Centre.

I travelled down to join in coaching sessions with Socrates.

To meet the legend in person was a delightful happening. Towering over me at six feet four, he did everything with huge energy and laughter. We took to each other immediately.

I couldn't compete with his drinking and he smoked heavily. He would talk politics for hours and his knowledge of Brazilian and South American history was encyclopaedic. His childhood heroes were Fidel Castro, Che Guevara and John Lennon. A courageous and big hearted man, he had persuaded his team mates of the Corinthian Football team to display Democracy on their shirts, challenging the brutal Brazilian military dictatorship of the time. He was fifty when he came to Garforth so his twelve minutes of playing as a substitute didn't set the world alight, but even at that age he could spray the ball around, though the crunching tackles of yore were gone. Socrates enjoyed nothing more than late night philosophical debate.

"The Greek word hedonia is translated as pleasure; let me fill your glass, that is taking delight in tangible things as well as music and the arts in general."

"Why not include moonlit nights, bird song, the light breaking through the trees at dawn and in the evening farewell to light and welcome of night.

How do you measure pleasure?"

"Hedonism is the looking for the condition of hedonia. The human organism is basically empty."

"But malleable?

"Yes we get our conditioning as we grow up, changing, monitoring our reactions to the social and cultural teachings of our mentors."

"Who are our mentors?

"Parents, teachers ."

"Dictators, propagandists, liars and crooks?"

"Yes, but we must sift through that dross to ferret out happiness. Kierkegaard said, *"the truth will set you free but first it will make you miserable."*

"Is there an opposite of hedonia?"

"There's always an opposite of everything.

Anhedonia is the inability to experience pleasure.

My oldest friend Isidoro, after a lifetime of joyous existence, taking pleasure in everything that captured his mind and vision now sits in a chair being fed and lost to the world."

"Yes, yes one of my old friends too has all the key symptoms of depression.

He was a man who could immerse himself in opera and tell you about every cast list and performance of the last fifty years. Now he doesn't even listen to opera on the radio.

His palpable delight in food, whether fish and chips or a gourmet production is gone, and his sexual activities a distant memory."

We drained the last of several bottles of Chianti and agreed, or I think we did that we might need to drop Prozac in the water supply and accept having a population wandering around with inane looks on their faces and sitting around their televisions dribbling and watching game shows and Top Gear.

Sadly Socrates' hedonistic life finally grabbed him by the throat and he died aged fifty seven.

> *"Piss well and be cheerful: that is the best one can do in this world."*
> **Frederick the Great**

When Shearer and Lineker and their ilk displayed their wonder at the lives many of the poor lead in South Africa during the World Cup, you wonder what they have been doing in their retirement except play golf and find new partners.

At least Mark Lawrenson now knows about Spion Kop and so do the lads back in the studio.

Football used to be so simple. When I played we had a Goal keeper, who was always a big geezer in a thick jersey who you could barge on the shoulder. Now if you as much as touch them they collapse in a heap and take ten minutes to recover.

Twenty guys run on to take a player off on a stretcher. Two seconds later and they're back.

In front of the goal keeper were a right back and a left back who never foraged forward beyond the halfway line or saw themselves as menacing attackers and creators of goals. They got stuck into the other team's wingers in the first seconds of the game.

Jock Campbell of Charlton once knocked Nat Lofthouse into the stands.

Lofthouse clambered back on and immediately scored a goal.

Campbell's infamous trademark sliding tackle would have had him off the field in the first minutes of a game today.

The manager's instructions were limited to "get stuck in" and on Fridays "to wear boxing gloves to bed." The coaches for the juniors were all old footballers gone to seed, pot bellied smokers who spent most of their time at the billiard table or down the betting shop. The trainer rubbed some oil on your damaged ligaments and pronounced you fit. Derek Ufton, the Charlton centre half and Kent wicker keeper suffered from a dislocated shoulder that would spring out of place on various occasions and leave him on the side-lines. He was in the dressing room with his arm in a sling when the Chairman Stanley Glickstein came in smoking a huge cigar.

He clapped Derek on the back "Well played skipper."

The first team trained for about an hour, rarely with a ball and then retired to the dressing room to smoke and play cards. Unless they were cricketers the players in the summer break were window cleaners, painters and decorators or got cushy jobs with one of the director's companies.

In front of the full backs were a right half, a centre half and a left half.

The centre half spent the game fouling and harassing the centre forward and never went up for corners or played the ball across and back to the keeper, never tried to be creative. A right winger and a left winger ran down the touchline whacking the ball across for the centre forward to head. Big solid balls with laces containing the rubber bladder that weighed a ton on wet and muddy pitches.

Centre Forwards had foreheads made of steel. We had a centre forward once who used to nut the changing room door open.

The famous joke was that in an international match Tom Finney kept crossing the ball for Tommy Lawton who scored a headed hat trick. Each time Tommy winced and held his head. Finney asked him why. "Well you see Tom, when Stanley Matthews crosses the ball he always delivers it with the laces facing away from my head."

Now some of you may have noticed I haven't mentioned inside forwards, especially inside rights. You see that was where I came in. I controlled the game. I was a liaison officer between the half backs and the centre forward and wingers, slipping the ball into space for them to run onto. Inside rights or lefts were mostly about five foot eight, stocky and elusive, a little cerebral, minds ticking over to gauge the right angle to pass or shoot, always aware of the position of other players. We were adept at the short pass and running into space, screaming for the return, even pointing to the spot where we wanted it. Equally a quick look up and a forty yard pass with either foot to the other side of the pitch was part of our repertoire. I practiced one move that proved successful time and again. Chasing a ball out to the touchline I would control it and set off at a fast pace. Out of the corner of my eye I would sense the defender getting ready to climb into me. I would then suddenly slow down as if unsure and as he came in to tackle me, accelerate away again usually leaving the defender floundering on the ground. I also perfected glancing a pass to a team mate off my chest.

I was the entertainer for the crowd who when I got fed up with flicks, back heels and laying on goals for others, I'd shimmy this way, weave that way, leaving four defenders in my wake, the crowd screaming "Go on my son."

I'd draw back the trusty left foot or the equally obedient right foot,

And bosh bosh, the goalkeeper was picking the ball out of the net.

No hugging or milking the crowd or silly dances.

I gave a cursory nod to the crowd. Shook hands with my team mates and with my head down, I modestly trotted back to the centre circle. I loved scoring goals but equally I cherished making them for others. I wanted to create passes of beauty that thrilled the crowd. I had a vision of the field and knew instinctively who to pick out for my passes.

The first game I ever saw was at Charlton. I got on the tram from Greenwich High Road and joined the good natured crowd making their way into the stadium.

Clutching my programme, a bag of peanuts, carrying a rattle and wearing my red and white scarf, I was hoisted on the shoulders of cloth cap wearing men with roll-ups in their mouths and passed down like a floating parcel on an assembly line to the front of the terraces to lean, panting with excitement against the railings.

I was stunned by the landscape. The deep dark green of the pitch, the white washed lines, the sun glinting on the corner flags. The row upon row of standing fans swaying and waving rattles, singing songs with tunes and funny words, not the obscene, inane or racist chants of today.

Suddenly the theme tune which in those days was the Sabre dance by Khatachurian blared out; I can still hear it thrumming in my brain today. Then these gods in white shorts, blood red shirts with white collars and red white hooped stockings burst out of the tunnel. I gasped and my heart beat faster as the crowd went mad.

The players pranced around like skittish race horses, doing little short sprints and breathing deeply. Later on the theme tune, to my regret was changed to When the Red Red Robin Comes Bob Bobbing Along, a catchy enough tune but without the excitement of Khatachurian. The player's images were encrusted in my mind.

I would dream of Charlie Vaughan, a craggy bow legged centre forward who could hang in the air for ever waiting for the cross to arrive and nut it into the net.

The crosser was usually Gordon Hurst, a balding fast right winger who sometimes instead of crossing would blast the ball into goal from an oblique angle.

Or more often over the bar. Billy Kiernan on the left was more subtle, a tiny mop haired player with only one foot capable of crossing the ball but accurately.

Harold Phillips was the "stopper centre" half, never leaving the back of the opposing centre forward for a second. Benny Fenton, a tricky right half with a deserved reputation for foul play. Later, a great crop of South Africans arrived at The Valley.

It was still possible then to combine a cricket and football career.

Stuart Leary was a very fine centre forward and an outstanding all rounder for Kent.

Sid O'Lynn not only played inside forward for the club but represented South Africa at Test level. Eddie Firmani was one of the first players to go and play in Italy, sold by Charlton for the then princely sum of thirty five thousand pounds.

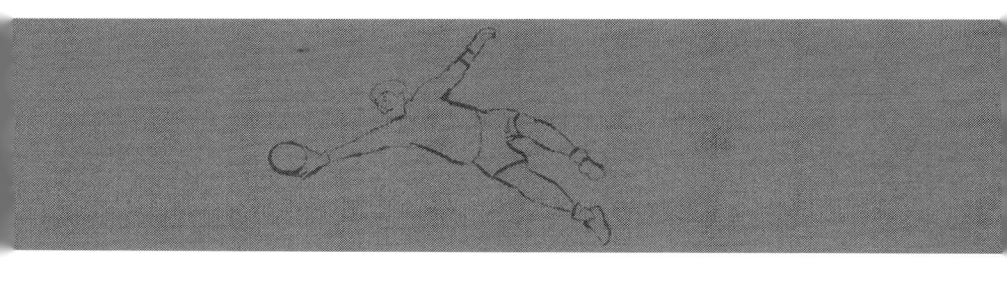

Sam Bartram

"If you are a Goalkeeper,
it doesn't matter what you save the ball with
if you keep it out — it's not a goal."

My idol from day one was Sam Bartram, the Charlton goalkeeper. Not because I wanted to be a goal keeper. His ginger hair, green jersey and burly figure dominated the goal area.

He would trundle into the goal to place his cap inside the posts.

I only saw him wear it once and it transformed him. He suddenly wasn't Sam Bartram but a guy in a cloth cap. They say goalkeepers have to be a little mad and eccentric. Sam fulfilled those axioms. He even took penalties sometimes, lumbering up and usually belting the ball over the bar. But he was a God, so it didn't matter.

Goal keepers then vey rarely threw the ball to a team mate.

The convention was to belt the ball as far up field as possible.

His mad rushes at the opposing forwards to divert or punch the ball off their foreheads were part of a ritual, the matador daring the bulls to get the ball into his net.

At the final whistle, nose streaming and my ears so cold I thought they had dropped off, I would rush round to get the great man's autograph, again and again.

He once asked me if I was selling them. The shock on my face made him laugh.

"No of course you're not son. I'm sorry." Was Sam Bartram apologising to me?

He once remained on the pitch as a thick fog descended. A policeman eventually loomed out of the fog to tell Sam the game had been abandoned and both teams had left the field. I arrived at Charlton just as Sam retired. He had been a miner before joining Charlton. They went from the old Third

Division to the top league and finished runners up in his first three years at the club. He played twenty two years for Charlton, winning an FA Cup winners medal in 1947. On my first day he came out onto the pitch whilst we ground staff boys were training and went into goal.

"Come on young man. Let's see what you're made of."

I was so nervous I kept hitting the ball straight at him.

"Loosen up son. Be natural." I then beat him ten times on the trot.

He grinned and put his arm round me as we left the pitch. In my dreams I can still feel his great hands on my shoulder. I was surprised when I later learnt he was only five foot ten. In my mind he was nine foot high like his statue outside the ground today. His creased face was always breaking into laughter, especially when I turned up with my Tony Curtis perm and drain pipe trousers. After a period in management at York City, Sam became a columnist for the People newspaper.

He died over thirty years ago but I sense his presence even now.

Maybe he's an Earth Angel.

Wilf Mannion was a small dainty figure who could conjure goals out of defensive mind-sets, would lift your heart and mind as he dribbled and cajoled the ball to his will. I saw him play for Middleborough against us a few times.

A true will of the wisp, he scored a sublime goal in one game mesmerising several players and running the ball into the net and I ran home dodging in and out of the crowds, dipping my shoulders, prancing through a gap and whipping balls into the net. I was Wilf incarnate all the way home and for months afterwards.

I played for Bermondsey Schools Under Fifteen team and we became the first Bermondsey Team to win a trophy, beating Woolwich Schools in a two legged final at Charlton and Millwall.

Because we played our home games on cinder pitches we garnered a fair amount of publicity.

Charlton asked me to join their ground staff; a ground staff boy in those days was the equivalent of an apprentice today. My daughter Sophie's partner, Gary Crawshaw, a talented and much travelled professional footballer, now a leading fitness consultant in Oxford, recently discovered by chance in a junk shop, a Charlton programme of a game between Charlton and Sunderland.

In a section called *Echoes Across the Valley* is written;

"Newcomer to the ground staff at the Valley is 17 year old Richard Morris, an inside forward who has greatly impressed in Charlton's colts this season." It goes on to say, *"Now he has the opportunity to develop his undoubted talent on the right lines."*

The Sunderland team sheet has the English international Len Shackleton at inside left. A unique talent, his career suffered after he headed a chapter of his autobiography, "What the Average Football Director knows about Football" and left the page blank.

The Valley ground then had a stand only on one side. The terraces were dotted with metal barriers. Urinals were made of corrugated iron with troughs overflowing on match days with the stench of urine, laced with beer. The ground capacity was 70.000. Inside its gloomy facade was a boot room and groundsman and billiard rooms. Two larger rooms were the visitors and home team changing rooms. The car park was a surface of cinders where we also trained on rainy days. I got five pounds a week and a day off to learn shorthand and typing at Woolwich Polytechnic. I had decided I would play for Charlton and England at football, and Surrey and England at cricket.

Then on retirement I would be a top sports journalist on the Daily Express or News Chronicle.

I swept the terraces and Marvin Hinton made the Horlicks. A young goalkeeper Tommy Sanders, later jailed for manslaughter, cut the grass.

We all whitewashed the lines and stuck in the corner flags.

After our work we trained by running around the perimeter of the pitch and hitting balls at the goalkeeper. Marvin was teacher's pet. He was the boot cleaning boy, meaning he kept warm in the boot room whilst the rest of us froze on the terraces and stands. And of course he was in charge of the Horlicks making, keeping us waiting for ever or pretending he had run out of supplies. Marvin was lucky in his physique, a languid passer of the ball, hardly ever getting injured and went on to a distinguished career with Chelsea. I only ever saw him again once on Croydon Railway Station and we had absolutely nothing to say to each other.

At one time I was loaned out to Bexleyheath and Welling, a non-league club, and played alongside my former idol, their player manager Charlie Vaughan.

Charlie had hair parted in the middle, a hooked nose, bandy legs and a calm demeanour. He was a magnificent support to me and encouraged and advised me for the short time I was there.

I scored a fantastic goal against Arsenal Colts at Highbury. I did a short corner with the winger, took the return, rolled the ball back like Puskas, deceiving the defender, bent my shoulder and went left towards the penalty area and unleashed a shot that sailed into the net from twenty five yards.

It was to no avail. Marvin Hinton got injured and with no substitutes in those days, we lost 4 - 1. I was the leading goal scorer for the Colts. Everything changed when I got badly injured against Chelsea Colts. It doesn't matter now, or so I say and think but of course it does. We had played at Chelsea's ground two weeks before. Denis Allen, a boorish professional from a well known footballing family introduced me before the game to a diminutive guy called Jimmy Greaves.

We had a little chat. His goal scoring exploits for Chelsea Colts were already legendary.

He proceeded to rub it in by scoring five of the goals in our eight nought defeat, crucifying Marvin Hinton in the process. I had nothing to be ashamed of, running myself into the ground and screaming at Marvin to get stuck in.

Jimmy as ever was gracious and modest after the game and said I had played well.

In the return Greavsie was not present, already having been promoted to first team duty. They still had a formidable team including Mel Scott, Barry Bridges, David Cliss and Peter Shellito.

Unfortunately for me they also had a thug goalkeeper whose name I have forgotten, yes honestly!

I had burst through the Chelsea defence when this nasty piece of work who had spent most of the game telling me he was "going to get me" leapt at me with no intention of getting the ball and smashed my knee. Today I would have probably been put back together but the blazered idiot manager was one Peter Croker whose only claim to fame was he had played in the Charlton team that won the FA Cup in 1947, told me to go out on the wing. I limped through the rest of the game and went back to Charlton's ground for the afternoon First Division Game, as all staff had to.

The trainer took me into the dressing room and had a look at my badly swollen knee. Stanley Glickstein the Chairman came through in his velvet collared overcoat and puffing on a large cigar. He asked who I was. The trainer told him I was a junior player and ground staff boy.

"He shouldn't be in the treatment room on a match day" was his comment and I was dispatched to the stands with a bandage wrapped around what was now a serious swelling. I was sacked by Jimmy Trotter the manager of Charlton and former England trainer and began my slide down the leagues. Whilst earning my living as a builder's labourer, Erith and Belvedere gave me some happy times including two goals against Romford in an FA Cup Qualifying round celebrated in the local Kentish Mercury with a cartoon caricature of me. I still have it. Our dreams of glory were soon shattered when in the next round we drew West Auckland in the dreaded North. We travelled by train and stayed in a hotel, the first time for most of the players. I delighted in telling the players to put their shoes outside the door overnight and they would find them polished and shining in the morning.

They were delighted to find that I did not speak with forked tongue.

The Auckland dressing room had a central stove with a few pieces of coal. Ice was on the inside of the windows. Their fans had spent the morning sweeping the snow off the pitch. The wind was piercing like hailstones against my cheeks. My mouth was frozen to a rictus grimace. I was so cold I passed out briefly at half time as I entered the marginally warmer changing room. Hulking great miners with huge knobbly knees, shovel hands and ruddy faces knocked us all over the place. We retreated to London 3-0 losers.

My ligaments had never recovered from the Chelsea tackle and I had started to predictably always go left, a bit like my politics. Before the injury I had the facility to go either way and shoot with both feet. My hamstring was always snapping and I began to dread letting the team down. I moved on to Faversham and Maidstone United.

My last hurrah before my surprising later comeback was with Beckenham United.

We played Charlton Colts and I scored the winner, a last gasp effort. Peter Croker was still the manager and couldn't, pigmy-minded as he was, resist sneering and taunting me during and after the game.

The rest as they say is history and I slipped into oblivion.

But never in my mind. With Wilson's help I was always making comebacks.

"It's in the mind Ricky, you're strong there. That's your place to be."

I went often to see him and have his special massage technique and words of wisdom soothe my mind and body. I loved the landscape, the tough and bleak moors and the verdant valleys where stone cottages nestled in isolation with sheep and cows standing in the fields, contemplating or munching.

My other life started to take over.

I'd be at Wembley for an England game and the tannoy would ask if there was an inside right in the stadium. Raising my hand I was rushed down to the changing room and swiftly kitted out. It was a crucial qualifier. In the first half I scored a goal with a terrific shot from outside the area. We went 2-1 down in the second half and with ten minutes remaining, I equalised with a header and then set off on a mazy dribble going past opponent after opponent to crash the ball into the bottom corner of the net to win the game.

That dream became the precursor to my comeback. A phone call from Bedford Jezzard, a former England and Fulham centre forward took me to Craven Cottage. Fulham was the beneficiary of my skills on many occasions.

One-two's with Johnny Haynes and Bobby Robson. I sometimes got on the end of crosses from Tosh Chamberlain if they weren't hitting the corner flag. Jimmy Hill never stopped moaning at me, even when I scored.

When I was approaching fifty I started to slow down. I lost the electric speed off the mark and being honest with myself, I chose to play as a holding midfielder as the current phrase was, like Bobby Moore.

The body was painful and creaky but the football brain was as acute as ever.

I hung about near the half way line and sprayed short passes, long passes all over the field, neat diagonals, chipped balls over the heads of opponents, dinks into the penalty area, clipping the short balls into space, taking the pace off for the player to sweep onto it and score. One critic said I could play for ever, so slow had I become.

The least intelligent of my team mates were unable to think quickly enough but the naturals, not necessarily Einsteins, but instinctive thinkers and movers, relished my contributions. I even scored a few goals sometimes, surprising the goal keeper with a chip over his head from thirty yards.

Wilson and Thelma

"It is the sport with a single starting gate and a thousand finishing lines."
"Accept that some days you're the pigeon and some days you're the statue."

I had taken up my pigeon keeping again and had a bevy of beauties.
Thelma, named after an old girlfriend was the star of my team.
I put her and some others in a wicker basket, delivered them to Greenwich Station and off they went to be in the Bordeaux to London Race. To my everlasting surprise and pride Thelma won. A whoosh and a flutter of wings, the panting heroine came through the hatch and posed quivering from all that gallant effort. Thelma was descended from a pigeon breeder's group in Belgium, at one time the cream of the pigeon racing countries. The famous Reuter's Press agency began as a pigeon service. Baron Nathan Rothschild used pigeons to gain advance knowledge of Napoleon's defeat in 1815 to make another fortune on the bond markets. I had first been drawn to the sport by Marlon Brando.

He and James Dean were my childhood film star idols and for a time I toyed with being James Dean instead of Denis Compton. In the film *On the Waterfront* a film about dockland corruption and also about McCarthyism, Marlon has a pigeon loft on the roof top of his tenement block. The tenderness with which he holds his pigeons and demonstrates their beauty moved me deeply as did the beauty of Eve Marie Saint.

I had started to visit Wilson more often and was able to warn him of my arrival by sending Thelma. Wilson fell in love with her immediately.

I would creep through the village, walk up the hill, cross the moor and arrive late at night. I told him of my aches and pains. His massage technique caressed the hard muscle and tension in my calves. I slept on a bed of straw and sheep's wool, with a fern pillow,

We got up at dawn for a run and a dip in an icy mountain stream.

We slept for an hour and then had our first meal of the day. Rough bread made in Wilson's brick oven, covered in a paste he made from herbs and berries he collected every day.

In the afternoons we swam and kick-boxed. Soup and more green plants from the hillside were our supper. Then with the fire stoked up and its flames sending shadows around the cave we talked. Oh how we talked. Wilson told me about his trips to visit Krishnamurti in India and California. Krishnamurti had resisted attempts to being deified by the cult of Theosophy. He had developed his own philosophy and built schools and centres in India, California and England.

The one in England is in beautiful countryside in Hampshire where one can eat three vegetarian meals a day prepared from their own garden and walk in rural peace and solitude amongst the indifferent sheep.

There was an atmosphere of slow-moving people carrying their thoughts around with them. No intervening preachers, but a library stocked with hundreds of books and videos by K.

The architecture is like a cathedral chapter house, made out of young oak and pine wood with one special Quiet Room.

The brochure advises you not to go there for the first day but to absorb the vibes of the building first.

"Meditation was the key to life" wrote K.

"What do we mean by becoming?

I am this and I want to become that and this becoming is a series of conflicts.

When I have become that, there is still another that and so on… why do I want to become something other than what I am?

Because of our conditioning, because of social influences, because of our ideals, we cannot help it, it is our nature… saying that puts an end to discussion.

It is a sluggish mind that makes this assertion and just puts up with suffering.

Would we degenerate if we did not struggle towards an end?

Of course we would. We would stagnate, go from bad to worse.

It is easy to fall into hell but difficult to climb to heaven."

Wilson was interested in Sports meditation techniques.

Its practitioners claim it relaxes the athlete's minds while increasing their ability to focus on performance. An American professor of neuro-science worked with the Dalai Lama on the brains of Tibetan monks and was astonished at their cranial capacity. He called them the Olympic athletes of meditation.

Wilson had run across the Sahara, up Kilimanjaro and raced across all the fells in the Lake District. Blessing was fascinated by the idea of Fell Running and I had promised to ask Wilson about it.

Wilson told me the first recorded fell race was in Scotland.

Malcolm Canmore the Scottish King who fought against and killed Macbeth in 1057 needed a swift messenger in the mould of Pheidippides at Marathon in ancient Greece. Fell races were organised on the premise that the runners would have the skills to navigate their way over difficult and hostile terrain with fearsome gradients whilst carrying the proper survival gear.

He emphasised the importance of the proper footwear, a trainer that was non-waterproof allowing the shoe to eject water and dislodge peat picked up from the soggy ground. Wilson was scathing about peak bagging in which the main ambition is to reach a coveted peak and claim the conquest. Some runners leave a business card.

"It can cause erosion and attract too many people intent on personal glory, There are too many people invading the sanctity of the mountains.
Come on let's run."

We scrambled across the rocks and Wilson like a bounding gazelle led the way up a very steep gradient. I huffed, puffed and groaning sat down.

"It's no good I can't do it Wilson."

Wilson came back and sat next to me, putting a consoling arm round my shoulder.

"Ricky, you're only temporarily out of condition and that makes you out of confidence too. Why don't you set yourself a target, there's no reason why you couldn't run a marathon or win Wimbledon."

"Are you serious?

"Of course, mind over matter, Meditation over muscle."

I wondered why he had never taken up tennis.

"I only like competing against myself, not an opponent."

"But you race marathons and other footraces."

"True but I never notice that there is anyone else in the race.

I am always so far ahead that my thought processes take over and only I exist.

That's why I have all the world records for medium or long distance running. I enter a zone where I can see the horizons of other cultures and the goodness, kindness and plenty waiting for all peoples and places if they give up greed and war.

That's what I am racing towards."

"A dream?"

"A vision that could become a reality?"

"Is that why you never stay for the medal ceremonies?"

"Yes. I am gone already in my mind. The body soon follows.

Ricky, I want to take you on a special journey with me one day"
"Where to?"
"I can't tell you now. Be patient and continue your career.
Something major is about to happen in your life."
He kicked the dying fire out, turned on his front and was asleep in seconds.

Wimbledon

*"If you can meet with Triumph and Disaster
And treat those two imposters just the same...
Yours is the earth and everything that's in it
And – which is more – you'll be a Man my son."* – **Rudyard Kipling.**

I returned to London and started thinking seriously about an attempt on Wimbledon.

I was nearly fifty and the back was just beginning its downward slide into constant pain. This could be my last chance. I managed to get through a load of qualifying tournaments and eventually was given a wild card. I think the committee saw it as a gimmick which is very un-Wimbledon but there was a boycott of the tournament that year by many top players and the authorities were desperate for something or somebody to attract the public. A grey headed, slightly paunchy fifty year old hardly seemed to fit the bill but I began to do all the exercises Wilson had given me. I gave up Havana cigars, red wine and meat.. My forehand was formidable but like a lot of club players my backhand often let me down. Drob agreed to coach me and I improved tremendously, whipping balls across court like him.

I had been brought up on grass courts at Blackheath Tennis Club and there had become a strong volleyer and server, quick to the net and nippy in retreat to the baseline. I was becoming more confident with Drob every day and looked fifteen years younger, even my hair taking on the blondish tint of youth, admittedly with some artificial aid.

My old friend Billie Jean King came to advise me on cosmetics and tennis. We had first met at Queens where I was a member. I was playing doubles on the wood courts with some rich advertising executives one Sunday morning.

As I came off the court, there she was waiting for a game, a diminutive little lady in glasses. She had just outed herself as a lesbian, with the attendant ghastly publicity of the corrupted tabloids. She looked bruised and forlorn but smiled and said "Hi guys. Had a good game?" The others left but we had a little knock about together.

I was in love with her from then on. She had enormous charm, laced with vulnerability and shyness. She was absolutely honest and courageous as a player and as a person.

Billie led the way for women's tennis and her uncompromising beliefs changed the future of the women's game for ever. She had been coached by Alice, though their personalities clashed at times but even Alice tells of sitting in the commentary box at Wimbledon with the Duchess of Kent when Billie came in and curtsied to her Highness before hugging Alice.

"Do you know Alice?" said the Duchess

"Know her? She taught me."

Billie and Blessing had become great friends. Blessing made her laugh with her irrepressible energy and often wild shots. Billie told us about two young girls she was advising, Venus and Serena who, she said, were going to take over the world of tennis.

The first round was easy. I played some low-ranking guy from Venezuela. Drob had done a load of homework on him and gave me a game plan. I also cruised through the next few rounds and almost by magic found myself in the semi-finals.

The reality hit home. I was being besieged by the press and fans.

Drob was calmness itself but something was missing and I was not feeling confident. I played a six foot four giant with a permanent scowl called Ivanisivic.

He had a service like an express train and I was just hanging in there at two sets to one to him. I sat in the chair and towelled my sweat streaked hair and took my mantra from my pocket, the exhortation of Admiral Collingwood before the Battle Of Trafalgar 21 October 1804.

"Now Gentlemen let us do something today which the world may talk of hereafter."

Luckily for me Ivan the Terrible was tiring and served a series of double faults.

Every line decision went in my favour and he became ragged, cross, red faced and smashed his racket into the turf.

It was all over in thirty minutes, the last two sets 6-1 6-0.

I was the first British finalist since Bunny Austin in 1938.

I slept well and awoke to hear that the world was going mad over my win.

I knew I had to see Wilson. Drob drove me to Yorkshire but I left him in a village nearby and walked to the cave. Wilson as ever was calm and solicitous trying to calm me down.

"To survive this test, think of all the preparation you have taken over the years.

Not so much the physical but the mental preparation.

Your wide reading, the thoughts imbibed of the great philosophers, the mantras chanted, and the evening communications with the Garden Gods.

Now is the time to think about the rhythms of the game of tennis, the way you move towards the ball, the size of the steps you take, how to prepare and anticipate the return. Remember the brain moves about so you must bounce around with it and weave from side to side in preparation before serving. You know your serve isn't that strong but you also know the value of placement. Swerving the ball away from the backhand so far you send your opponent so wide he can only send it back with a superhuman effort. But you go in so quickly and volley away the ball. Top spin, back spin are all shots you can execute but all will come down to mental strength.

Go to your zone from the first second of the match. Think of Walt Whitman and his phrase *"singing the mind electric."* Enter the space and stay there until the final shot proclaims your victory."

"I thought you didn't care about winning."

"Let's say for this long wait by the great British public, I will make an exception."

I live a brisk ten minute walk from Wimbledon. I walked along Wimbledon Park Road wearing a wide brimmed hat I'd bought in The Cancer Research UK charity shop in Putney High Street where Karen worked as a volunteer. No-one recognised me. It had been a perfect fortnight, the sun shining every day. The houses along the way rent out their frontages to shirt sellers, badge sellers and food and drink vendors. I strolled along already locked in my tennis player's zone. This was going to be it I was sure, my day, my destiny. Billie and Drob were waiting. Billie was already in tears; Drob, phlegmatic and calm. I stepped out onto the court in hot sunshine and to a mighty roar from the crowd.

My Russian opponent looked nervous and in the knock-up I tested him with some lobs and drop shots. The first set was cagey and I sensed the crowd's fears.

Were they again going to be robbed of a glorious victory for the home boy?

Could Fred Perry be finally forgotten?

I couldn't quite press home any advantage I had.

The crowd's patriotism sat on me like a heavy and sweaty blanket.

My legs were leaden, my back ached, and my heart was going far too fast.

My doctor had prescribed beta blockers for my atrial fibrillation but it was as if they were having no effect. My mouth was dry and I seemed to have double vision. The Russian won the first set and I took some time to come off the seat for the second set, earning a warning from the umpire.

The Russian began well but I fought back remembering Wilson's advice on my serve. He had said I should go out as wide as I could into the tramlines and hit the ball with such swerve and spins as to force my opponent into the first row of the spectators stand. This tactic runs the risk of leaving a wide area of the court for the opponent to hit the ball into. But though my backhand was weak, my forearms, developed in my time as a builder's labourer could be compared to the mighty Rod Laver.

The strength of my forehand was devastating the Russian. Wilson had prescribed a very precise swivel of my hips that had no extravagance and exerted little strain on my lower back. I took the set and then piled on the pressure, feeling the longer the game went on the less chance I had of winning. Some of my shots were sublime and have become part of the folklore of Wimbledon.

One outrageous retrieve from way out in the tramlines, a ferocious but graceful forehand from the back of the court and a top spin lob are still remembered by fans.

I won the next two sets, and raced into a five-one lead in the fourth. The Russian was demoralised by my dominance and the baying crowd but found some strength from the depths of his Russian soul and fought back to 4-5.

I was serving for the match, for the ghost of Fred Perry, for England, Britain, London and my birthplace, Wimbledon, for sporting immortality. The game was titanic. Back and forth the ball was driven with the Russian chasing every ball, the cheers and groans of the crowd, a chorus to the history of Wimbledon.

It came to pass. Match point. I looked up at the player's enclosure. Karen, Tessa, Sophie, Blessing, Sheila and Edith were clinging on to Billie.

Drob was feverishly chewing gum and above them I saw the ghost of Lew Hoad.

He was knocking back a bottle of white wine with a beautiful girl on his arm and gave me the Imperial Roman thumbs up. He was laughing his head off.

One serve, one perfect serve and it was done. I bounced the ball amidst a complete and utter silence. As I threw it up, the wind swirled and I lost balance.

Raising a hand to apologise to Ivan I thought of Wilson in his cave in Yorkshire.

I began the ritual of the throw-up again. The ball fell onto the racket and I struck it perfectly and with direction as far to the forehand of my opponent as possible.

He made a superhuman effort and returned the ball to a gasp from the crowd.

I came in and made the perfect volley. Somehow he returned the ball again.

I had to race back and retrieve it, sending the ball into orbit.

He smashed it back and I was already at the net and sent it skimming away into the far corner and into the history books and the folklore of tennis. I don't remember much else but I do remember Karen bringing me breakfast in bed and asking how my back was.

I went onto our roof terrace and declaimed the response of Henry the Fifth to a present of tennis balls from the king of France.

"When we have matched our rackets to these balls
We will, in France by God's grace play a set
Shall strike his father's cross into the hazard
Tell him, he hath made a match with such a wrong heir
That all the courts of France will be disturbed
With chases."

The squirrels didn't seem impressed with my oration and the snails still attacked that evening in wave after wave of attritional warfare as if at Agincourt, on my newly planted cosmos sonatas.

They were the days of glory, of wine and song, of dreams come true.

Wilson's training and advice, the support of my friends and family helped me to join the immortals.

Part Four

Football Comeback and Glory

"If at first you don't succeed try, try, again."

My fame was such that no-one seemed surprised when I announced my football comeback with Tottenham and scored fifty goals in the season. For the next few years my goal tally was only surpassed by Greavsie who became a great mate. He was a football genius and a very funny fellow.

I was picked as a last minute choice, the oldest player at fifty four years of age ever to play in a World Cup. And joy of joys it was in England where in 1966 we had triumphed against West Germany.

I played well within myself in the early rounds and watched with pleasure Owen scoring my type of goals and Sheringham making my kind of passes.

Gazza was ebullient, buzzing and sober. I loved the guy; there was something about his spirit and presence. I never guessed that he would become a tragic operatic figure, a Pagliacci, a clown with grease paint and tears running down his cheeks like mascara, an idol, who fell from the heavens so far and so fast, shattered into little pieces and broken by the sporting gods.

Who would have thought there were so many tears in him?

Bobby Robson kept patting me on the back, shaking his head in wonder, asking for my advice. "What system do you think we should play Ricky?"

He was a passionate man whose syntax never kept pace with his enthusiasm. His warmth overwhelmed you and I never saw him refuse to sign an autograph or fail to acknowledge a fan's greeting or inquiry why he wasn't playing the fan's favourite player. Pearcy was mad, a wild eyed oak thighed nutter who never drew back in a contest, didn't want to know about tactics, believing a big heart was enough.

The country began to get behind us and I came in for a lot of praise for my contributions. "Old man Ricky can still do the business," was one headline.

Saga and Age Concern approached me for advertising promotions and The Prime Minister held me up as a hero of our times, the living proof that it was never too late.

I was an icon for the young and a vindication of right living for the old, he wrote in *The Guardian,* much to the disbelief of my family and friends.

I thought I might have to miss the semi-final as I had teaching commitments but the PM intervened and the local authority kindly let me off teaching *18th Century Life and Culture* for two weeks.

"Ricky will play!" screamed the newspaper headlines.

I got up early and finished *The Leopard* by Giuseppe di Lampedusa, about the tenth time I had read it. The book hypnotises me. The characters are so authentic and fascinating and the book has a dream like air, melancholy moments interspersed with laughter and excitement

"If we want things to stay as they are, things will have to change," says the handsome but impecunious young Tancredi to his uncle, the world weary Don Fabrizio, Prince of Salina in a Sicily on the cusp of Italian unification.

The film of the book is a masterpiece by Visconti. Alain Delon is stunningly handsome, energetic and affectionate as Tancredi.

Claudia Cardinale is sexily beautiful and seductive as the prize for the fading dynasty offered up by the "new-made man" her peasant father.

Lancaster bestrides the film like a colossus, the very epitome of Lampedusa's portrait.

I had some Weetabix, yoghurt and toast and fed the cats.

Karen dropped me off at the Tube entrance. It was her woodcarving class that day so she didn't come for the game. Both Sophie and Tessa sent me good luck cards but preferred the tennis at Wimbledon as they had Centre Court tickets.

I got the tickets as a former champion and was happy for them to be there. In the semi-final against Germany as foretold by the sages, it went to penalties and I was the last one of the penalty takers.

The team couldn't look as I took the long and lonely walk to the penalty spot.

I picked up the ball, looked at the goal and thought it's nothing,

"Just ten yards Ricky my son."

My technique was to place the ball on the spot and whilst doing so to look intently at the point to the right of the goal keeper, making him think that was where I was going to place it. I then hit it as hard as I could to the left. The ball tore into the net and I was a national hero. I was extraordinarily calm. Whilst the lads went mad. I kept saying "It's not the Final, calm down, there's a long way to go."

The day of the World Cup Final against Argentina, my back was very sore, after all the garden had had to be watered and swept and the flowers deadheaded.

I regretted the two bottles of red rioja and half a pound of mature cheddar cheese I'd knocked back the night before.

I'd been give special dispensation to sleep at home by the manager and after feeding the four cats I went by Tube from East Putney to join the lads in the hotel for the ride to Wembley.

It was warm but not sultry, thank heavens. The trainer gave me a couple of paracetamol and I took my diabetes and heart pills.

In the dressing room everybody was quiet until I inspired them with parts of Shakespeare's famous St Crispin's Day speech from Henry the Fifth as I wound bandages around my various weak points and poured White Horse Oil embrocation on my aching limbs.

"That he which hath no stomach to this fight,
Let him depart;
We would not die in that man's company that fears his fellowship to die with us. This day is called the feast of Crispin:
He that outlives this day and comes safe home will stand a tip-toe when this day is named."

Still trailing some bandages I stood on the edge of the bath for the final exhortation.

"We few, we happy few, we band of brothers; for he today that sheds his blood with me
Shall be my brother... and gentlemen in England now a-bed shall think themselves accursed they were not here, and hold their manhoods cheap while any speaks
That fought with us upon St Crispins Day."

The lads were shouting and gesturing and Gazza paraded around in his jock strap beating his chest yelling;

"Once more into the breach or close up the wall with our English dead.
Cry God for Harry, England, and St George"

We sang our own World Cup Song to the tune of *Money Money Money* by Abba. Everybody had perked up.

Rio suddenly threw me the Captain's arm band. I protested but he insisted.

"Ricky you're the talisman, man. Lead us to glory."

As we stood singing the National Anthem, tears poured down Gazza's cheeks whilst the rest of us stood impassively, inside our own cocoons of emotions.

Bobby was singing his head off, his chest stuck out, immaculate in suit and tie, eyes glistening with tears.

I have to admit I was nervous and I gave the ball away too easily at first.

Gazza had his name taken and even Teddy was off the pace with his passes.

The Argentinians were pulling every trick to get Gazza sent off and some of the tackling was horrendous. However it worked against them. I took a free kick from twenty yards out floating the ball onto Gazza's head.

He knocked it down to Michael Owen who slammed it home.

At half time we were subdued but feeling more confident. Nerves were going to play a part and we all inwardly, I think, prayed for there to be no penalties to settle the game. The second half opened with a lightning strike by Argentina to equalise and as the game wore on I felt tired. We were all flagging.

Bobby asked me if I wanted to be substituted but I shook my head.

With three extra minutes to go I found myself inside the Argentinian half with no support and four players in front of me.

Some primeval memory spread through my ancient limbs and I set off towards goal flicking the ball past two defenders, sidestepping another and nutmegging the fourth. As the goal keeper rushed towards me, I stepped over the ball, feinted to go right and went left and slid the ball into the net. I fell to the ground as I was engulfed by the team. I could hear my name being chanted all around the ground.

Ricky! Ricky! Ricky!

Bobby was hugging me and Gazza just kept repeating, "Awesome."

I could hardly walk up the stairs and dimly heard the Queen say "Well done Ricky."

"Can you manage the weight of the Cup or do you want a hand dear?"

I must have passed out when I went down the steps for when I came round Karen was passing me a glass of red wine and saying "Well done Ricky, the garden looks great."

Gardens

"What wondrous life is this I lead...
Meanwhile the mind from pleasure less
Withdrawn into its happiness...
Annihilating all that's made to
A Green thought in a Green shade." – **Andrew Marvell.**

Gardens play a large part in my life. After we had to leave Maze Hill and its relative grandeur with a Breakfast Room and a Study, and its large and abundant garden, we were sent to a halfway house by the local authority, sharing accommodation and cooking facilities with other families.

We were allocated the conservatory, ample enough for my mother, me and two sisters. It was a very large Victorian house with leaded lights, mahogany doors, oak fittings and a Gothic gloominess. In the kitchen there was a rack with bells and the names of the servants in gold letters who still ghosted around its echoing corridors.

I imagined them saying "Coming Ma'am" or my favourite thought, summoning up in my mind, a haughty butler and crinoline wearing ladies tiptoeing to the door.

"Your carriage waits without Ma'am."

The garden was superb, let run wild with huge rhododendrons and lilac bushes and plenty of space for ferocious football matches and gentler cricket games.

I was born less than a mile from where I live now, grew up in and love London.

I always told myself that wherever I lived I must have a space where I can get outside, even if it was just a balcony.

I was very lucky in love, family and friends and we all share in the delight of light, flowers, laughter, cats, dogs and companionship at table.

I have lived for the last thirty three years in Wandsworth.

My garden is where I ponder, plan or just ruminate, sitting sphinx like with a glass of red wine gazing at its beauty, the ever changing patterns and combinations of the shafts of light. We have a large frontage and the containers on the wall are protected by a wooden picket fence. Lobelias, green miniature trees, trailing fuschias with red drops of blood-like flowers bursting through the fence.

When people stop to look and comment I am filled with pleasure and a little pride.

Leading out from our writing and workshop room upstairs are French windows onto a balcony where in summer, geraniums predominate with cosmos sonatas, dwarf holly hocks, wall baskets with yellow mimulus and scopia leaping out from the wall.

I first saw oleanders in Crete and never thought they could survive in London. But now, bought locally there one is towering in a large green barrel, its pink flowers, a bonus from the Mediterranean.

A grape vine climber is also a new addition doing well. The down stairs garden can be reached by a spiral staircase from the balcony. This area is where I go over the top and plant feverishly in April and May, as many as five hundred plants each year; with clusters of petunias four feet across, hardy and trailing fuschias, my beloved Bizzy Lizzies or impatiens. There is an impatiens called noli me tangere. The exhortation "do not touch me" Christ gave to Mary Magdalene as she stood astonished before him at the Resurrection. I think of these long lasting summer flowers as alleviating impatience, my impatience if I think they are taking too long to flower. There are many varieties which arrived as stowaways on trading boats from Africa or in the cuffs of trousers.

In the beds are hydrangeas, evergreen bushes, astilbe, cineraria, and Mexican blossom. Many years ago, a plant fell over the wall from our neighbour like a gift from the garden gods and we have enjoyed a massive Tree Peony with yellow flowers in April ever since. Tucked around the corner in an alley are huge tomato plants and courgettes.

We are blessed with quiet, every day sounds, bird song, comic and affectionate cats, curious foxes, clever and industrious squirrels and invading snails and frogs; good neighbours and privacy.

Towering weeping firs, beech, sycamore trees shield us from God's wrath and our neighbours back gardens. When I still haven't decided on my back four or bowling attack, I spend several hours doing as Voltaire's Candide advised;

"Cultivating my garden."

All tremors of the heart and mind disappear, at least until kick-off time, or the first ball is to be bowled, the first serve to be sent down.

It is here that I make momentous decisions on my next comeback, or tactics for the next game, sometimes repeating my lifesaving mantra with Leonard Cohen's help.

"There's a crack, a crack in everything, that's how the light gets in, that's how the light gets in."

At times I feel my heart is going to burst with love for my family, my world of books, flowers, music and sport. I ache for those who have gone from us far too soon, particularly Stephen, a precious nephew of thirty four. I ache for those yet to be born.

Filling my thoughts are the unsteady, the unfulfilled and the empty ones, unable to retain their curiosity, thinking endless travel to distant places and paper backs bought at airports, empty chats with other blank minds are going to carry them through the vale of challenges, disappointments and excitements that make up our blocks of existence, our tilts at the sport of life.

I feel for the walking wounded, bandaging their broken dreams in ghostly wards, resounding with pain and distress, where uncaring attendants fail to hear our pleas and exhortations.

"O Lord, hear our pleas and let our cries come unto thee."

Ten, twenty years glide by and many of us are still repeating the same old clichés, "Yes you told me that." We talk but don't listen; a mask of false concern without comprehension or genuine sympathy.

Desperately hoping someone will arrive to assuage our pain, gild our dying days with gold, silver and mercy.

"Come unto me all ye who travail and are heavy laden and I will refresh you."

God hasn't arrived yet and maybe never will. But don't tell anyone.

They won't be able to handle it.

Millions of us cherish the rituals of religions.

Life goes on. Or does it?

Blessing and I once played in a tennis tournament in Wales and on the way home stopped at the Cistercian Tintern Abbey in the Wye Valley. The valley is enchanting with a few houses sending up wispy smoke from their chimneys and a view of the River Wye ambling along.

We knew and loved Wordsworth's *Ode to Tintern Abbey* with a line that always brings *"thoughts that lie too deep for tears;"* for both of us;

"Those little, nameless, unremembered acts of kindness and of love."

As we stood in the evening sunlight, I thought of the destruction of these divine citadels of prayer perpetrated by a vengeful and greedy King and his henchman Thomas Cromwell, who might have pondered on his actions as he laid his head on the block on Tower Hill in 1540.

His legacy was the Dissolution of the Abbeys, and the theft and scattering of the stones for secular purposes.

"Bare ruined choirs where late the sweet birds sang," wrote the supreme writer in the English language, William Shakespeare of Stratford upon Avon and The Globe, London.

The "sweet birds" he refers to were cowled monks gliding from library or dormitory to worship in a daily round of prayer and song.

Thomas Morley wrote in 1592 that the object of religious music was to draw the hearer in chains of gold to the consideration of holy thoughts. The monk's days began at 2.am for Matins, the night office and were completed with Vespers at 4 and Compline at 6pm.

The calefactory was where the monks could warm their hands before entering the scriptorium. Books have never been cherished so much since the Middle Ages.

The monks and lay scholars saw reading and learning as shafts of light and spent hours illuminating the manuscripts of animal skin with gold. Perhaps in a world threatened with Viking Raids and in darkness for much of the time both metaphorical and real, the monk's exquisite and painstaking work gave them a peace and reverence long since lost in our modern world.

The simple meals they ate were prepared by lay brothers, monks who had not taken Holy Orders.

The ideals and aspirations of men who erected structures half way between heaven and earth and created a Gothic art tinged with mysticism and fantasy are articulated here. Men were still looking inward and upward for solace and direction.

An Abbey is a frame for a mystery. The main founder of the Cistercian Order, St Bernard of Clairvaux who re-affirmed the Rule of St Benedict criticised the fierce lions, centaurs, gargoyles proliferating in churches' architecture, believing it took the monk's minds away from the contemplation of the works of the Almighty One. Gothic churches are swept by shafts of light, filtered by stained glass windows. Untutored peasants, weary from their labour in the fields could read and comprehend the Abbey as a sermon in stone and glass.

Despite the main purpose of an Abbey being the worship of God, the Cistercian architects were great artists and provided every comfort for the monks.

They followed the *Cistercian Rule* which states;

"The monastery shall be built if possible (I like the humility and the gracious hesitancy of the Rule) in such a way that it contains within its walls everything necessary, to wit: water, a mill, a garden, and workshops for the various crafts so that the monks need not go outside. Barns and farms shall be spread across the Abbey's lands. The herds of large and small animals will never go further than a day's journey from the barns."

Every need was provided for. The Choir for prayer and chant song; The Chapter House for the daily reading of *St Benedict's Rule* and the place for discussion of the necessary daily upkeep and problems of such an enterprise.

The Parlour was the only place the monks might converse in and where the daily assignments for field work were given out. A Lavabo or fountain for washing or drinking led to the Refectory. There was even a Cellar for the making of beer and wine. When the time came to join their Maker, a cemetery received their bodies wrapped in a simple winding sheet with neither coffin nor tombstone to mark their passing.

I watched as people took photographs like modern pilgrims, begrimed by travel and engorged on food, gawping at this flawed and ancient ruin, encrusted with grime, its centuries old prayers embedded in blocks of stone, most of them unaware of the ancient lives buried around them which had been sustained by a belief in everlasting life.

Blessing wondered whether we could ever grasp the immensity of the past. I told her I thought only if we could emulate the monk's way of life.

To be able to lead such a contemplative and rigorous quotidian existence is a many- splendoured gift. Brave, chaste, and holy, men acting like unarmed knights in shining armour, tilting at windmills with only their puny fists, chasing fabulous, fire spouting monsters into the bowels of hell.

We left feeling stronger, braver, and cleansed.

Blessing posited that the rituals of sport today precede the rituals of religion. People wear the favours of their team not pilgrim's badges.

Holy Communion takes a few moments as does five times a day obeisance's to Allah. But sports rituals can, I argued, like religion, shut out if only temporarily the ache in the veins, the dolorous trail of tears, and the devastation of unrequited love.

I thought of myself as a child at Royal Hill Primary School when I went to the store every Friday to find a pair of football boots to fit me for Saturday's game on Blackheath or in Charlton Park. I took them home and cleaned off the dried mud with a hard brush, dubbining them. Dubbin has been used since medieval times to soften and waterproof leather boots. It is a combination of natural wax, oil and tallow.

I then washed and whitened the laces, cut tags from old cleaning cloths to hold up my football socks and begged my mother to iron my shirt and shorts. I loved the sound of my studs, tapping tapping as we waited in the tunnel or ran across a metal grid in the park, our young bodies leaping, dodging, and doing short sprints before the battle began.

What of the sheer joy of dribbling past the full back to cross a ball into the penalty area? What of the exquisite ecstasy of cracking the ball home, the net billowing and leaving the goalkeeper disconsolate, the fellowship of the field when an opponent came up to you to say "Well played mate."

I loved the continuous banter on the coach on the way home; the singing, the sense of being at one with your team mates.

We have that unique essence for such a short time and don't apprehend that we will never savour the moments again. Football is so much faster than cricket; ninety minutes of crazy endeavour, insults, flying tackles, referee's admonishments, and physical exhaustion; penalties, bookings, injuries and broken hearts at the final whistle, flashing past like a speeded up film of the Keystone cops.

To read today, the inane and pathetic excuses from managers and players is dispiriting.

Ferguson and Wenger are just two examples of whinging beyond sense or comprehension. The spare and scholarly looking Wenger never sees the foul that leads to a penalty for his team even if it is committed ten yards outside the penalty area. He sees it very clearly when it is a penalty against his team. His team only loses because of poor refereeing decisions.

The ruddy faced, choleric and at times childish Ferguson is a disgrace with his comments when he loses and a prime cause of the niggardly fouls, disrespect for referees and parlous state of the behaviour of players and fans alike. His players Ferdinand, Rooney and Evra are sneaky bits of business when it comes to fair play and as for the retired Gary Nevile, who is even worse as a malevolent commentator, words fail me.

The banal chorus has now been joined by the lugubrious, sad-faced Kenny Dalglish still I fear burdened by the horrors of Heysel and Hillsborough.

"The wee fellow was fouled all through the game. I just want the same treatment for everyone." Now Ferguson and Dalglish have stained the game even further with a poor handling of a sordid fracas, racial strife rearing its ugly face again.

The pantomime villains, Suarez and Evra, refusing to shake hands like children in the playground, sparking pages of comment in the papers and on television. I would absolve Harry Redknapp from my criticism. "Arry Boy" still has the old fashioned approach to the game;

"No, fair enough the boy done well to even get there but I think it was offside in all fairness to the referee."

He delights in the skilful player but is too polite to dismiss the serial moaning offenders like Ferguson and Wenger for what they really are.

Both managers draw the curtains when it comes to confronting what football has become, the plaything of rich multi- millionaires who are masters of the dodgy deals that bedevil the game and buy and sell players like commodities. There are owners who rarely appear at games like The Glazers of Manchester United.

The system produces disloyal human beings like Carlos Tevez, a greedy mercenary and an unintelligent spoilt child who acts as if he has lost his dummy.

A club with a sense of morality would have sent him packing long ago.

But an Arab paymaster controls from afar whilst soaking in unearned oily riches seeping from the ground in Abu Dhabi and draws back from sacking him and doesn't support his manager, Mancini.

The import of foreign players has brought some amazing talent to Britain but in doing so the game has lost its soul.

Most of the young millionaires just want more, don't want to win for the pride and the loyalty of the fans but so they can up their value on the transfer market and sell their bodies and faces to advertise perfume, groceries and pizzas on television adverts or in magazines.

An example of going over the top is Andre Villas Boas whose relative youth doesn't excuse his banalities. The current Chelsea manager, after a poor run by his side, celebrates a victory by laying into critics for their "persecution of Chelsea" and praises his players for giving everyone "a slap in the face."

"They deserve a respect they don't get."

He stumbles along digging himself into deeper mumbo jumbo and ridiculous hyperbole.

"There is a phrase that is interesting."

"The person that you are is a triumph in the person you want to be"

He has been reading too many Christmas crackers fillers.

But the really sick stuff he reserves for the end of his Zen-like thoughts on the result of a single football match. Whilst myriads of people are dying from war and famine; whilst good men and women toil away to help their fellows; whilst Angels weep and devils work their evil, this sad little fellow taking home a couple of million pounds a year says of his victory.

"This was a triumph in human values."

Go to Somalia, Palestine, The Congo, Mr Villas–Boas, and bend the knee to real people, not to overpaid footballers and foul-mouthed fans and greedy directors.

Get a book list and read about the OTHER World. Get a life based on reality.

It's probably too late for him. He is of a different generation and unable to use language in a coherent and humanistic way.

We have come a long way from annual fixtures that used to be embedded in the national mind like The FA Amateur Cup. Clubs like Bishop Auckland who won the Cup ten times. In 1955 they played in front of 100,000 fans at Wembley, the last occasion an amateur game attracted such a crowd.

We have come even further from Albert Camus, author of L'Etranger and La Peste and the goal keeper of Racing Universitaire d' Algiers,

"What I know about morality and the duty of man I owe to sport; "Sticking up" for

friends, valuing brave and fair play."

I'm afraid a world long gone, long gone, Albert.

Too existential.

Okay, enough already you might plead, but why are so many of us disillusioned with football?

And why do I cling onto cricket as the last repository of chivalry and fair play? Especially as we have just jailed three Indian cricketers for a betting scam.

My Cricket bat was an icon, treated with reverence, oiled with linseed, my batting pads whitened and pristine, torn and battered batting gloves worn like medals from the battle front. Respect for opponents, for the umpire, for the spirit of the game, applauding fine shots and centuries, well taken catches and opponents as they left the field. I am moved when Freddie Flintoff kneels down to commiserate with a shattered Brett Lee, his great paw placed gently on the bowed head of a vanquished opponent, a benevolent Caesar granting him a laurel leaf of peace.

The ebullient Australians Laver, Roche, Newcombe clapping an opponent's shot.

Cliff Drysdale, an affable South African at Wimbledon, deliberately missing a shot to give his opponent the point because he felt his opponent had received a bad call previously. Who would do that now?

Think of the inspiring sight of Bobby Moore and Pele, exchanging shirts and looking at each other with respect and love for each other's skills and sportsmanship.

In the modern games we will never see their like again. I want to puke when Ferguson or someone compares Rooney to Pele. Rooney is a thug and a greedy one. His lumpen skills don't get even close to Pele's grace and charm, let alone his supreme skills.

As for sportsmanship, forget it.

A snarling, nastily aggressive persona is Rooney's image.

I always thought that a man of the integrity and hard upbringing of Ferguson would never succumb to the blandishments of distant billionaires and the posturing of Rooney to up his salary.

I confess that the vulgarities of McEnroe and Connors, the grunts and groans of the Williams sisters, the petty tantrums of lesser players upset me.

The crowding around the referee by footballers contrasts with the immediate acceptance by Rugby Union players of a referee's decision.

Football crowds rejoice in obscene and ugly baiting of the opposition.

What sort of "fan" taunts Manchester United players about the Munich Disaster?

What sort of fan taunts Liverpool about Heysel and Hillsborough?

The sight of drunken bare chested Newcastle fans in temperatures below freezing singing filthy songs says a lot about our society.

How can Chelsea fans salute the utterly vulgar and insincere John Terry?

The proliferation of tournaments and cups in all sports means a relentless diet of sport throughout the year. The Premier League clubs claim fatigue for their players at the end of the season but can't wait to take their teams to Japan or Africa or anywhere some money can be made, some shirts sold.

Kevin Pietersen claims he wants to spend some time with his new child but will haul his carcass anywhere when the money sign comes up.

"In the good old days" the changing seasons meant something then.

The cricket season meant cut grass, spring flowers, song thrushes, the tinkle of tea cups as the evening smell of dusk and dew descended.

The ball became an enemy as some big bottomed giant loomed out of the gloom and hurled the ball through the air.

Did you play the forward defensive stroke, or the block shot that might produce a single to cover or the leg glance for two?

Or did you take a chance and drive through the covers for four.

If your confidence and eye was in, what about a twirl of the hips and a hook over long off for six?

I loved the cut shot, the pull to long off. I loved the scampering for a quick single and snaking my bat into the crease. I was doing the reverse sweep before it was invented.

I could throw a ball from the covers that whacked into the keeper's gloves like a pistol shot or took the top off the bails like a hedge trimmer. Watching masters and natural gentlemen like Tom Graveney or Neil Harvey was to sit in a golden cloud of reverie and rejoice that the gods had created cricket and such consummate players.

They didn't make batting look easy, they made it look natural and joyous. Sometimes my eye could only see the arc of the back lift before the ball arrived at my feet on the boundary.

Most cricket grounds allowed spectators to sit on the grass which encouraged camaraderie as we young ones played impromptu games at lunch time.

The rituals of cricket are like no other game in the world.

The taking of a guard is discussed by the knowledgeable crowds.

"He's taking middle and off to counter the spin."

The techniques, "I don't think he "middled" that and he hasn't been middling it all day"

"I'd call that an off cutter, but he can swing it both ways."

"It was an arm ball." The ritual of the drink breaks. Spectators stand up and shake legs which haven't been in action for several hours. At Lunch out come the cork screws and bottles of wine and exotic sandwiches of smoked salmon, cream cheese and olives from hampers containing proper wine glasses. More prosaically, pork pies are prised from a Tupperware container and large beakers of beer are consumed in vast quantities.

Tea is taken and the thermos flasks are opened and the fruit cake or biscuits offered around. Or maybe the wine must be finished with the remaining smoked salmon.

The whole ground stands for a century or a haul of Michelle Pfeiffer, a euphemism for a five wicket haul. "Fivefor" Get it?

I was made captain of the fourth eleven at St Olaves's Grammar School, the Latin master and cricket tsar thinking if he made me responsible for something I would stop disrupting his class and learn to translate Cicero. To both our surprise it worked.

I didn't get the cane or any detentions that term. I can't say I mastered Cicero but I did come top again in History and English and even earned a blue ink comment from the headmaster instead of the usual red. After three ducks in a row I demoted myself to number nine. I was a fearless close catcher and took so many that I justified my place. I only put myself on to bowl if all seemed lost.

My slow donkey drops lulled sensible batsmen into extravagant strokes. They either missed the ball altogether or wafted a catch to square leg.

At school, silly mid-off was a place of honour for me. I once got struck on the temple fielding there and fell back clutching my head and saying to the Latin Master, now reincarnated as an Umpire, in my best Laurence Olivier voice "I've had it sir."

He gazed quizzically down at me, "I'm afraid not Morris."

I'd ended up at St Olaves because my mother wanted me to go to University and they taught Latin there. In those days you had to have Latin to be accepted at a University

I took the train from Blackheath Station and walked down Tooley Street, taking in the smells of the river and docks, molasses, tobacco, tea.

Big men with bursting muscles in cloth aprons, heaving barrels and crates onto lorries, fags in their mouths and expletives filling the air. Wafting from the grimy cafés was the smell of bacon where the men could buy bread and dripping for a penny and a full breakfast for a shilling.

From our classroom windows we could see Tower Bridge and the Tower of London, and barges low in the water, weighed down by their heavy cargoes.

The pupils were an eclectic mixture. Posh kids with smart blazers, shiny shoes and immaculate sports kits from Weybridge and Surbiton. Tough kids from Bermondsey wearing black plimsolls and dirty collars who got sent home until they could come properly dressed. I was somewhere in between.

Neither posh nor glottal London, our impoverished circumstances in snobby Blackheath meant my mother struggled to cope with the school's demands.

She made me a blazer which had a peculiar jutting out collar and a lopsided badge.

I spent the first few weeks fighting kids who sneered at my outfit.

I wasn't a good fighter but I was dogged, so they gave up in the end, influenced by my prowess in playground football.

Masters wore gowns and swished around like mad vultures in pursuit of their prey, the schoolboy carrion.

We marched into assembly in squads of six and sang

All Things Bright and Beautiful and *Onward Christian Soldiers* whilst the patrician Headmaster, M.A Cantab watched us like a malevolent god, malignancy etched into his forehead, his imagination already swishing the cane on some juvenile bottom.

If you were late, RCC Carrington gave you a choice. Two whacks of the cane or learn a poem. I learnt a lot of poems.

We wore caps outside school and devised ways of getting them further and further back on our heads. In the non-school environment the teenage fashions of the day required some cash. I coveted a duffel coat and a corduroy jacket and Slim Jim ties with a rolled collar on my silk Billy Eckstine shirt. Pencil slim drainpipe trousers and a duck's arse haircut completed my appearance.

To pay for them I got up early to do a paper round and after school delivered beer, cordials and wine to the wealthy of Blackheath Village.

Football Pundits

"A person who professes to have actual or self-professed authority."

Adrian Chiles is a typical example of someone elevated beyond their capabilities. Perhaps he should have stuck to playing the double bass or guiding the fortunes of his father's scaffolding business.

A bubbly Billy Bunterish figure he gives the impression of sniffing the air like a bear before selecting his victim and bringing his affable side into play.

On television he comes across in a deliberately understated, faux innocent manner, defying the studio crowd to break his cool demeanour.

There is an element of pleading to be liked if not loved. If you call him late at night he will either be watching football archives of West Bromwich Albion or mugging up on every statistic, no matter how trivial on the game. He was miffed to be messed around by the BBC and took the ITV job with glee. His greatest asset is his true love of football and his puppyish pleasure in its frailties and triumphs.

Kevin is the same, a very similar character. He was never a great player but made himself by force of character and determination into a very very good one.

He is sentimental to a fault which causes him to make choices and predictions that come back to bite him up the arse. But his heart is huge and honest.

Gareth was an honest yeoman as a player and manager.

He is articulate and accurate with his assessments and comments.

I can see him coming back as a manager one day and being very successful.

I like Edgar Davids too, because he never tries too hard to be clever but is obviously a shrewd student of the game. Andy Townsend is sharp and pleasant, albeit liable to show his temper from time to time when disagreed with.

Andy loves playing with the technical aids, demonstrating theories on why some players perform better than others in certain areas, the breakdowns in defence, the lack of awareness amongst the forwards.

I once played snooker with Lineker and Hansen in the BBC club room and felt the cold wind of celebrity breath every time I turned my back, even though I was the only one there to have won a World Cup Winners medal.

Lineker's fresh faced charm has gone with time, his face shrinking and leaving prominent nose and ears covered by a leathery tanned face and a permanent eyebrow twitch as if playing Eric Idle's character in Monty Python.
"Nudge Nudge, Wink Wink, know what I mean?"

Hansen is still the best looking commentator in the game but his summaries are squeezed out in world-weary manner and bored rhythms. He reached the pits of the commentary cesspool when he said of Mandela's appearance at the World Cup Final "He can be truly proud of what he's achieved."

No sense of the magnitude of the man, a man who makes men like Blair, Bush and Brown look even more like the liars and pigmies they are.

The maxims sound tired and clichéd. Lineker's coy flirting with Hansen as they enjoy their special relationship is cloying and they don't make me laugh anymore.

As for Mark Lawrenson, he has the air of someone condescending to comment from his lofty perch on the stupidities of inferior players, hands folded discretely over his paunch and plainly bored to be trotting out the same old clichés.

Let us draw a curtain, a thick one over Alan "Robotic" Shearer, condemned to stumble through the same routine for ever, desperately trying to twist his features into some kind of intelligent and thoughtful mien whilst stumbling through his contributions.

Cricket Pundits

My garden life has been enhanced by Test Match Special. As I water or deadhead flowers or just sit with a book, I love the talk, the slowness and intricacies of the game, the descriptions of the movement of the ball, the changes in the field, the crowd pictures painted by the commentators.

Trevor Bailey always sounding as if he was in his cups and probably was.

"Straight ball hit stumps out" was often his pithy response to a fallen wicket.

I was once invited into the box and the empty bottles were lined up under and on the table. Freddie Truman went downhill very quickly after early promise to be direct and honest. The worst mistake a commentator can make, that is talking about himself and how different it was in the past was Fiery Fred's forte. He spent most of his broadcasting career saying,

"I can't understand it, no long off. Line and Length, Line and Length."

I could do without the irritating Boycott with his ludicrously exaggerated accent and boastful outbursts, "My Granny could have hit that with a lolly pop stick."

"When I batted…" His false bonhomie and desperate desire to be liked by the other commentator's grates on the ear.

As unfortunately does the recently recruited Michael Vaughan. Very knowledgeable but trying too hard to be witty. I think maybe there is still hope for him.

CMJ is an officer and a gentleman and a gentle and shrewd commentator.

Brian Johnson was a jolly and warm clown and I never tire listening to him giggling with Agnew over the Botham dismissal. Jonathan suggested that Botham, "had failed to get his leg over." Johnson struggled for a few minutes, gamely battling on with the commentary before collapsing into the giggles and the famous appeal to Agnew.

"Oh Aggers do stop."

Aggers is like a puppy dog granted the run of the whole park but has no real flow and poetry in his remarks, but he is good on the quality of the cakes sent in by devoted listeners. Vic Marks sounds like a public schoolboy, a giggler and prankster but shrewd in his assessments, especially in his journalism.

As for Blowers what can one say "old thing?"

"Another red bus goes down the road." "We now have six pigeons perching near our box." "A delicious cake from Mary in Sussex, thank you Mary."

I tolerate him as I would the village idiot. I hasten to add that I mean with kindness and civility. I have warmed to Simon Mann. He is genuinely knowledgable and in love with the game and unafraid to tease and cross swords with "the Boycott."

I also enjoy Phil Tufnell, very apt and knowledgeable and at times witty.

"Tuffers" plays too cutely sometimes the illiterate clown role with Henry cast as the erudite ring master; maybe Henry is, but he overdoes that mock claim to stupidity beloved of the privileged in our society, especially old Etonians.

"I don't understand either, old thing."

I miss the relegated Mike Selvey with his erudition, that and his acute reading of the game. Luckily I can read him in the Guardian. Another Guardian favourite is Frank Keating whose utter love of most sports matches my own. I feel we have been travelling the same road for over fifty years.

Frank can write of "the wireless" and carefree days at Lords with panache and wit.

The best television commentator of all time was Richie Benaud.

Richie was always quietly authoritative and never intruding, verbose or boring.

John Arlott

The Radio King, the doyen of doyens was John Arlott.

No-one comes near to his unforced poetic comments spoken in a soft country burr, his grace and genuine devotion to the game and its participants.

I was at Lords for his last broadcast and wept with many others as his voice came over the tannoy. It seemed like and was the end of a very special career.

This was a man in every sense of the word and I felt a kinship with him like no other.

He was a person with an interior life, possessed of a hinterland of wisdom and knowledge. John was a wine connoisseur, a poet, a sergeant in the Hampshire Constabulary. He stood as a Liberal candidate in Epping Forest twice.

Fate was cruel and kind to him.

Slated to cover the Manchester United game in 1958 in Yugoslavia he was replaced at the last minute and thus escaped the Munich air crash that killed twenty one people, including the immortal Duncan Edwards.

But he was devastated when his son Jim was killed at twenty one years of age driving a sports car his father had bought for him.

A typical sentence from one of his commentaries was about a shot from Clive Lloyd, the West Indian cricket captain, "The stroke of a man knocking a thistle top off with a walking stick." His epitaph on his gravestone in Alderney is from one of his poems

"So clear you see those timeless things that like a bird, the vision sings."

I had come to admire him from an early age.

In 1968 I was at Lords for the Test match against Australia. John was standing just to the left of a sight screen. I went up to him and introduced myself. I wondered why he was watching from there instead of in the commentator's box.

"I like to see the game from different vantage points and perspectives." In the course of our chat I told him I was going to South Africa for the first time to meet my wife's family.

"I hope you're prepared for the life there. I was shocked the first time I went when I was asked to fill in an immigration form stating my race.

I wrote "Human Being."

It's hard to imagine a more horrible system. Grown men called "boy," black nannies nurturing white babies and living at the back of the house in dark and gloomy one-roomed huts. In the shopping malls there were separate doors for the post office, the toilets; separate buses for the blacks. The streets were full of overweight men in khaki shorts and long knee-length socks and solid Afrikaner women interspersed with the pretty English-speaking women. John went on to explain in detail the system of apartheid and how it applied to cricket.

"Imagine segregating people in a game like cricket. Separate cricket leagues, separate facilities and areas reserved in the grounds for the blacks at Test matches which were between white teams only. Grass pitches prepared by black ground staff for spoilt young white South Africans to strut their stuff on. Blacks play on coconut matting pitches if they are lucky, more often on stony pitches littered with rubbish.

It permeates a man's soul, grinds him down and makes him lose his respect for his fellow human beings. Ask Basil." I turned to see Basil D'Oliviera, the tall rangy attacking batsmen whose late cuts and cover drives were strokes of freedom and glory, envied by anyone who played or watched cricket. He was also a fine medium pace bowler. It was 1968 and the Basil D'Oliveira Affair was occupying acres of space in the press.

"An honour to meet you, Mr D'Oliveira."

"Call me Dolly."

"How come you are not getting ready to play?"

"Yes how come?" said John.

"Colin came up to me in the nets and in his usual creepy manner told me I am to be twelfth man"

He did a very good imitation of Cowdrey.

"Dolly look old chap, I say, I mean we all know how well you did at Old Trafford and you're bound to be disappointed but we're giving Barry a chance. More penetrating a bowler don't you know? You'll be back before the season's out, believe me."

"Bloody liar" said John "They are trying to get you out of the way so you won't be picked for South Africa. What a coward Cowdrey is.

He knows Vorster and Allen are closeted in the committee room plotting to get you out of the way. Let's go and get a drink." He took us into the commentator's room and opened a bottle of 1960 St Emilion and we all soon felt better and optimistic. John had been instrumental in getting Dolly a job as the Middleton professional in the Lancashire League, kick starting a career that led to Basil playing for England.

In South Africa he was classified as a Cape Coloured. As the wine flowed he relaxed and told me of his first experiences of Lancashire weather and the difficulties he had with playing on grass. He spoke movingly of the warmth and friendliness he and his wife Naomi encountered in Middleton. "Our landlords were marvellous, our neighbours too. In the time we spent there I never had a racial incident or insult offered, at least not about my colour, only my bowling or fielding. It took me some time to stop trying to find the coloured entrances into pubs. When I went to the railway station to go to Lancashire I kept looking for the coloured only carriages. I spent my first night in England at John's flat. He worried whether I had a pullover and enough money to get by with."

At the time of "The D'Oliviera Affair" John wrote "MCC have never made a sadder, more dramatic or potentially more damaging selection than in omitting D'Oliviera from their team from the tour to South Africa." More pertinently and presciently he also wrote "Within a few years, the British born children of West Indian, Indian, Pakistani and African immigrants will be worth places in English county and national teams." He might have written at another time that white South Africans took full advantage of Scottish mothers or Welsh grandfathers. Tony Greig, Alan Lamb, Strauss, Prior, Trott, Robin Smith, Pietersen and so on.

Basil was lucky to have John as a friend. A quiet man until later in his career drink made him a more vociferous and aggressive character, he became caught up in the moves to isolate South Africa from international cricket and sport in general. To his huge disappointment the Tour to South Africa was cancelled by the former Nazi, Prime Minister Vorster because of Dolly's selection.

Later on D'Oliviera went on to score lots of runs, take hundreds of wickets, coach Worcester and win a permanent place in the hearts of cricket lovers.

John Arlott retired to Alderney in the Channel Islands where he gradually empited the contents of his fabled wine cellar, often in the company and with the assistance of Sir Ian Botham and Mike Brealey, dispensing bon mots, cricketing wisdom in that famous country burr.

In vino veritas.

R.I.P John

Fashions

I was one of the first bearded footballers. Early man didn't shave. Or so we believe. Every year another discovery tells us that early man was more intelligent, more adaptable in working out his environment that we can ever know.

The Romans shaved or was it just the rich who could afford barbers?

The first doctors were called barber surgeons.

"Hair cut, shave and was there something else needs snipping sir?"

Caesar and Augustus were clean shaven if we take the evidence of their busts in Museums throughout the world. Perhaps once they came in direct contact with barbarians, full beards became fashionable. The Emperor Hadrian we know from his busts spread across the Roman world had a beard. Perhaps as the Empire declined the Romans wanted to reassure themselves about their virility and courage. Victorian and Edwardian men covered their faces in hair as they subdued most of the world.

Perhaps they were trying to hide their shame at their racism.

The hirsute football players of the 1970's and eighties had mullets which have been defined as "business at the front, party at the back."

Football players have never been leaders of fashion but have just followed slavishly the pop stars and models. Now we have throwbacks wearing bandanas and Alice bands while those who know they are on the way to becoming bald, shave the whole scalp off. Bobby Charlton, a magnificent player but a sadly deficient director of Manchester United, taking the money from greedy mavericks and silent in the face of the blatant commercialisation of his club and the game in general, for years combed his paltry locks over his bald pate, deceiving no-one but himself.

I watched his debut at Charlton with the immortal Busby Babes when he scored a hat trick and commented "he's a bit one footed."

I am working with Kate Moss on a new range of football gear for the European Championships. Kate's a lovely girl if a little addled and inarticulate from time to time. I have designed a tank top that finishes at just below the nipples, leaving the navel exposed and ready for a gold ring piercing in the belly button. The shorts will be very short at the front revealing the beginning of pubic hair. At the back they will be longer to the calves leaving the thong and crack in the arse exposed, especially when a player is injured and lying down on the turf. Kate calls them the arse thongs. She's thinking of forming a pop group with that name, The Arse Thongs.

It looks like I may need to design a range of snoods for the wimpish footballers of today. Footballers running out in snoods to protect their greedy necks, I can only avert my eyes. The name Snood was originally applied to hairnets worn by single women in The Middle Ages.

Tights? Do me a favour! – Gloves!

Keith Weller of Leicester once wore white tights, a fearsome sight.

I wouldn't have been seen dead in gloves or tights when I was young even in winters of snow and freezing conditions, let alone on a football field.

Religion, Substitutions and Fouling.

"Manna From Heaven or self-professed authority."

Frank Lampard, whenever he scores looks to the heavens to dedicate the goal to his mother, who sadly died from cancer. It is a rare occurrence for it to happen when he is playing for England.

I am not aware of any English players crossing themselves before or after a game or when being substituted. Of the Germans I only saw Boateng performing the action.

Apparently Ouzil recites the Qu'ran during the German National Anthem.

As befits a nation that suffered for its Protestantism in the sixteenth century, the Dutch do not have many devotees of the rapid movement of hand across the heart and chest. Amongst the South Americans, Africans and Spanish an epidemic has broken out, Drogba is a serial crosser and the Argentinians are always topping up their chances of Paradise. Maradona looks up at the screen to check he is being seen performing the rite and hopes it is being beamed to the football loving Pope.

What the Pontiff makes of the idolatrous acts of celebrating a goal I can't imagine but maybe he adopts the *"Render unto Caesar what is Caesar's and unto God what is God's"*, dictum. The players express themselves in a variety of ways. Most have very little imagination, leaping on each other as if entering a brothel for an orgy.

Many goal scorers want a moment of glory all to themselves, running away and avoiding the rush of the pack of grinning hyenas, kissing the shirt or pointing upwards to the heavens, meaning I suppose that God scored the goal.

Then they allow the maker of the goal a hug and all disappear in a welter of bodies.

Lots of kisses, sometimes full frontal lip kissing whilst buttocks are clasped.

Again what His Eminence makes of this I can only conjecture? Players sometimes leap the barriers providing a surreal moment when they disappear from view to re-appear surrounded by security staff.

They don't take their shirts off very often since FIFA directed it was a yellow card offence. Roger Milla of the Cameroons started a trend with a dance next to the corner flag and since then we have had Abba style and shaking hips dances.

Unexpected player substitutions are often met with a glare at the touch line as their name is raised, a cursory nod to the replacement, a fingering of their rosary and a frantic double crossing of the chest. They ignore the manager's outstretched hand. When they finally reach the bench, a water bottle is picked up and hurled to the ground rather like a baby throwing its milk bottle and dummy out of a pram.

Someone replaced with about ten minutes to go to save him for a rainy day ardently kisses the substitute, embraces the manager, high fives the players and staff on the bench knowing the match is won.

Over the years the art of fouling and reacting to being fouled has become an art form with some serious Academy Award winners. The really, true fouler tries always to commit his crimes on the blind side of the referee, especially at corner kicks where it is open warfare. Holding, tugging shirts, elbows smashed into faces, blatant trips mostly go unpunished except for the free kicks always going the goalkeeper's way.

A truly great fouler will raise his hands above his head after a particularly vicious tackle, quickly telling the referee he was having his shirt tugged, theatrically miming the act. He also clutches some part of his anatomy unconnected to the tackle and goes down in simulated agony. Currently I would say Van Bommel of Holland is holder of the Golden Globe of Thuggery. Some of the greatest exponents of being fouled are forwards. Ronaldo stumbles, appears to regain his balance, and then tumbles over four or five times. Drogba goes down like a log. The game is stopped and he lies there absolutely still as if waiting for a shroud to be placed over his stricken body.

Anxious trainers rush on and anxious minutes pass whilst spray is applied in waves of fumes. Finally the wounded warrior is dragged to his feet or taken off on a stretcher. A substitute starts to warm up only, lo and behold and glory alleluia, he arises like Lazarus and returns to the fray, crossing himself several times.

God moves in mysterious ways his wonders to perform.

Is double crossing to ensure The Great Intercessor in the Sky will whisk you up to heaven if you die after scoring?

Do the Elysian Fields await with places reserved for you in Our Saver's Team?

He plays in goal but is always on the look out for goalscorers so Heskey and Rooney don't apply, for the time being we hope in Rooney's case.

Part Five

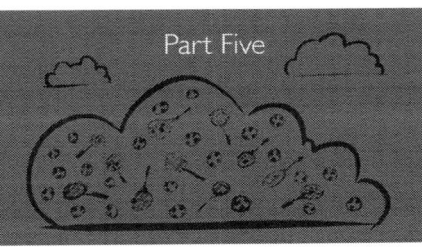

The Heavens, Big J and Me

Can't thou, by searching, find out God? – Job 11.7
Speak to the earth and it shall teach thee. – Job 12.8

How do I know so much about the heavens?

I realize I must tread softly for I tread on so many dreams. It will be impossible for many of you to understand my relationship with Big J.

I treasure my talks with him over the years and admire his perseverance in the face of impossible odds and the misunderstandings between Him and his Father.

I can only relate as honestly and openly as I can what has transpired, inspired and disappointed me in our discussions over the years.

I hope by recounting my experiences I can contribute to the common weal.

All our travails need to be sifted for the messages they may contain and to keep our curiosity pistons oiled and pumping so we can parcel out our energies to make life as fruitful and positive as possible.

How did I get into such a privileged position to visit the Heavens?

Well my Friend and mentor Wilson you will recall was granted the secret of everlasting life. Later he revealed to me that his contract with the Galaxies included a free travel pass to all parts. Any time he had to have some money it appeared in his hand and if hungry, manna dropped from the heavens. On rare occasions he was allowed to take a guest up there so I had the great privilege to go with him a few times. Our method of travel was a mystery. I had to sit quietly wherever I happened to be, and close my eyes. A fluttering of mighty wings, hands grasping my shoulders and arms, a gentle whisper in my ear, "Be with us Ricky today in Paradise," and I would be transported effortlessly to the Gates. On arrival, it is comforting to find Peter sitting on a Rock. He's quite grumpy but processes your visitor's credit card, reads out your rights and required behaviour whilst visiting. You will only see those people Big J says you can see and talk to. Certain areas are off limits. Explanations of the workings of the Lord are at His and His Father's discretion. Once great revelations are made you are bidden not to ever use the knowledge back on Earth.

I don't know so can't tell you if you meet up with long lost loved ones when you die, or what the punishments consist of down below.

Travel within the Galaxy is by a hanging rail. Just put up a hand and grab the rail and shout out your destination which is above like the maps on the London Tube. Everything is suffused in a green haze with thousands of colourful birds flitting and swooping onto trees and to my delight sitting on shoulders.

Angels fly from place to place carrying messages or mentoring the newly arrived.

I did learn that there are many angels on Earth. They are people chosen by Big J to stay on earth after their death to spread love and help to the sad, afflicted and those close to despair. They take many guises and you often feel you have seen them somewhere before. If you think you feel a consoling hand on your shoulder in the supermarket or a smoothing of your brow as you lie sweating and sorrowful in bed it will be an Earth Angel.

There is a constant temperature of 70 degrees. Communal showers send out continual rainbows of water. It takes some time to feel at home there. I kept seeing so many familiar faces who I would have loved to chat to.

Big J is very much a man of the people. He is tall, well over six feet, slim, very dark skinned with black piercing eyes and black hair and beard edged with grey. If you look closely you can see lines etched into his face. A group of Twelve Angels are at his immediate command. They are utterly charming and sing a cappella or to their own harp and guitar accompaniment.

A constantly changing group gives concerts daily. Louis Armstrong, beaming out that life giving smile often leads a group in scat singing. The urbane and elegant Duke Ellington directs from the piano. Thelonius Monk sits in silent contemplation whilst Miles Davis and Charlie Parker improvise on *Ain't Misbehaving*. Fats Waller brings the house down with *Your Feet's Too Big*.

One time when I was there the Maestro Giacomo Puccini conducted *Tosca* with Maria Callas. I actually got to talk to him about *La Boheme* which he said was his favourite opera. I was tongue tied in front of the genius Signor Verdi. Beethoven, Rossini, Mahalia Jackson, Lena Horne, Shirley Verrett, Vaughan Williams, Judy Garland and Nina Simone, when she's not in bad temper are just a few of the artistes I met.

Big J laughs when I ask him about the great painter's depictions of Him.

"Caravaggio came close and one of Holman Hunt's paintings reeks of authenticity, a real smell of the East. I love Millais' *Christ in The House of His Father* because it is so inauthentic and ridiculous. My Father looks like someone from Surbiton, John the Baptist is creeping along as if he is a thief in Docklands. My own favourite is Dali's but it makes me shiver with the bad memories it brings back."

"If I may say so my favourite painter is Piero Della Francesca, Big J."

"Ah, tell me why."

"Francesca's painting of "Your" baptism by John the Baptist has so many parts and nuances. Two young men are facing each other in natural poses. One gently pours water over the other. They seem as if they have come out of the desert and are recognising the days of drugs and parties are over. It's time to grow up.

The pretty girls are wide eyed and open mouthed. The hills and paths stretch out into the distance suggesting new departures. I'm not sure if the figure taking off his gown is representing You before the baptism or is it another young man seeking the Way, The Truth, The Life in the ritual cleansing of baptism?

The colours are muted yet luminous, the benign presence of the Holy Dove presiding over the ceremony, imposing silence and contemplation on the viewer. I stand in front of the painting in the National Gallery and can't explain its power over me.

Francesca's famous painting of Your Resurrection from the Tomb has an equally powerful but different impact. The only criticism is on technical grounds. The soldier on the right looks as if he is leaning on air as he sleeps. The four soldiers one feels have fallen to sleep out of boredom.

But "You" have been through the ordeal of crucifixion, you look confident and here you stand like an Emperor of all you survey. Eyes on the horizon, your stigmata displayed as a badge of honour, your ruptured body now healed, upright and formidable. Somewhere in front of you is the Kingdom you will claim to rule. I can hear the trumpets sound, the angels singing. No-one can deny your triumph over death.

"O death where is thy sting? O grave where is thy victory?"

Big J was impressed. "Steady on old chap, you'll be a believer next."

"When Chairman Mao was asked what he thought the effects of the French Revolution had been, he replied "It's too soon to tell" Big J.

Can I ask you a question about…?"

"What?"

"Your early days… you know, I mean what were you doing from say three to thirty, the start of your ministry?

"Oh I had a good time as a young boy. We very young boys went swimming in Lake Galilee with some of the mixed blood Palestinians."

"Mixed blood?"

"Oh yes. Lots of the Roman soldiers had Palestinian concubines. Their children wrestled, boxed and raced against us. Once a month we held swimming races. That's how I did the walking on water miracle."

"What do you mean?"

"Well when we waded out to the start line, I discovered by chance a sand bank which led into the water. I never forgot its location and used it later to impress Peter and the disciples. You look shocked"

"Well… loaves and fishes?"

"Oh that was well organized. We had advance warning that a great crowd was coming to hear me speak. I spoke with our patron Joseph of Arimathea. He arranged for a great shipment of fish from Lake Galilee and hundreds of loaves from the Galilean bakers. We put up a tent, stored the provisions inside and every time a basket was sent back empty, disciples filled it up, gave it to me and it was distributed amongst the multitudes. Ricky, the miracles are only meant to be symbolic, like the parables.

We wanted to teach people that if you share there is always enough for everybody. No-one needs to go hungry in the abundant world.

He reminded me that Christ isn't his surname. "It's a title, means "the anointed one."

"I was called Jesus Bar Joseph or Jesus of Nazareth as a boy."

"We had a big family. My family goes back fourteen generations, to Adam to Abraham, David and Solomon.

One of my brothers was a tent maker like Paul of Tarsus. James was in the oil business"

"Oil?"

"Olive oil. James was very clever and experimented with all sorts of blends. I helped him make a delicate nutty oil to make fish taste better.

The Romans couldn't get enough of our oil. James made a pale green one to soap their pampered bodies with here and in Rome. There was one I remember well, a golden green for meat dishes. There was no more beautiful sight in our land than a grove of ancient olive trees. I loved the silence and the solitude.

While I pondered on my coming ministry I'd sit amongst my brother's trees with a beaker of wine.

When the Romans destroyed a grove to build another barracks they sowed the seeds of our rebellion against their rule."

Big J regularly visits other Galaxies and makes friends very easily with devotees of other faiths. Gandhi is a particular friend. A real giggler, he tells Big J that he likes him but not his followers. "Your Christians are so unlike you."

Big J replies "Maybe commitment to me means not being a Christian, a word that carries so many burdens of history and horror."

My Father isn't Jewish. He's Everyman and Everywoman. To make anything work He has to have the qualities of a Chameleon. When black people pray to Him they visualize a black face, Asians a brown face and so on."

Big J automatically understands every tongue though even he can't remember whether the daily language of first century Nazareth was Aramaic, Hebrew or Latin.

He smiles and says, "we'll have to wait for Mel Gibson to explain it all."

There are hundreds of committees working on medical, philosophical, scientific and religious issues. Wilson is an honorary member of the Longevity Committee.

Tommy Cooper is Master of Comedy, always summoned on bad news and dark days."

"Lighten our darkness we beseech you O Tommy", sing the Angels.

Big J and all the disciples follow the cricket and football results, even Accrington Stanley's.

The Heaven and Hell Champions League constantly changes personnel.

No red cards or yellow cards are issued. He just sends you below. A first offence is a year's residence in the nether regions, the first offenders Division One where no punishment is given, except reading Jeffery Archer's books, so you could argue that is severe punishment.

A further offence means Division Two in Limbo where compulsory reading includes reading Top Gear by Jeremy Clarkson. Well at least they don't have to talk to him. Persistent recidivists are transferred to the Devil's Reserves and eventually to the First Team. No going back from there I am afraid. Lucifer is a fiendishly hard tackling overlapping full back with a snarling Gary Neville expression who occasionally sends gusts of his fiery breath to scorch the opposition. He has acquired many hard men over the years. Billy Bremner, Jock Campbell and awaits impatiently Nobby Stiles, Norman "bite your legs Hunter" the sneaky and thuggish fouler Johnny Giles and scarfaced Tommy Smith.

There are plans too for matches against other galaxies as travel visas become easier.

The Flying Saucer Company of Mars is negotiating with the UFO's on Venus to build an Air Bus together. Big J wants a triangular tournament played on neutral ground, the Moon, though stability could be a problem. He's got Galileo working on it. Another problem is the Earth's movement, which is the speciality of Galileo. He grumbles he doesn't want to start that nonsensical argument over again and be apologised to 300 years later by the Catholic Church.

Eventually, we are told, when God comes to gather his jewels, all will be revealed, pain will be overcome and the Fruits of Life will descend on the world or that part of the world we know.

God has promised Big J that an attempt will be made to disenfranchise all the fanatics, from all the faiths, starting with The Christian Right. "What do we want with Evangelical churches in the United States who have signs on their lawns saying Jesus Hates Muslims? The tele-evangelists are an abomination, hi-jacking me or my Father to their inanities. How dare they take my name in vain?"

The Zionist Ultra Orthodox Section has separate facilities and signs forbidding entry to the unrighteous. It also has separate entrances for men and women. Little girls dying before their time are made to cover themselves from head to toe on arrival lest the lascivious Hasidim are tempted by their bodies.

Apparently its presence is tolerated because it was a special dispensation from the Father but Big J wants the ruling reformed.

Big J shakes his head when I pass on G.K Chesterton's aphorism;

"How odd of God to choose the Jews. It isn't odd His Son was One."

"Look. Moses was tired from all that walking in the Desert and didn't sleep well in those forty days and nights on the Mount. The oral law my Father gave him became muddled in his mind. He'd already smashed the tablets in anger and destroyed the golden calf. He was no youngster and was emotionally in turmoil.

My father had given him a third tablet which he broke on the way down and left lying on the mountain. When my Father asked for two new stones to be hewn they both forgot about the third one. It's still there. Moses lost the plot.

He had selective hearing. All those Old Testament prophets were the same, stubborn and mulish in their dispositions.

What my Father actually had said is,

"I refuse to choose one nation above another for that way lie tears and recriminations but since you are such a stiff necked people, I will give you a non-renewable lease written on this tablet. The lease is until 1948 whilst you sort out somewhere for the tribe to live that doesn't displace another tribe.

I command you to make proper use of that time and create a harmonious community."

It was a one chance lease and they didn't take advantage of it.

Moses and my Father still argue about it."

Big J can get very animated on the subject of his Father

"I went through Hell for him. Have you ever been at a Crucifixion? No? Well let me tell you it isn't just a question of the nails. There's a reason we get the word excruciating out of crucifying. I hung there for at least twenty four hours then they broke my legs with an iron club, the weight of my body caused my lungs to collapse so I was virtually asphyxiated. I'd only had sour vinegar to drink and no message from my Father."

"No wonder you called out *My God, My God, why has Thou forsaken me?*"

"Yes. That's when He offered me the deal."

"The deal?"

"If I would hang on for another few hours without complaining he would abdicate in my favour when I got to Heaven within a short space of time."

"And?"

"A short space of time! Two thousand years already and he's still clinging to power.

Not enough that I was scourged, beaten and flayed until my blood stained the floor, then my body torn apart on the Cross. My life has been traduced.

The Jews claim I'm a Gentile, the Gentiles claim I'm a Gentile. Where were the Jews when I needed them? The bulk of the sects accept my divinity, the Quakers stay stum, sitting in their silences, I feel excluded. The Unitarians deny it. Most of them get confused about the three in one deal. We have had centuries of synods and falling outs. Let's say it one more time. God had Mary inseminated with his seed through Gabriel.

"Artificial insemination?

"That's where the mystery of religion becomes the mystery of life and the mortals draw back. CS Lewis wrote *"I believe in Christianity as I believe that the sun has risen. Not only because I see it, but because by it I see everything else."*

"Gabriel approached her at the Annunciation."

"Nunc Dimittis," I murmured softly

"Yes," sighed Big J. "a shock for my mother. And of course Joseph, a good man, who accepted the decision which was relayed to him by God's top official Archangel Michael.

Thus God is my Father. Mary is my mother. The Holy Dove is a wise old bird from the Sinai who lived through the Flood and I am as you see a fairly normal individual.

I do have special powers but for the foreseeable future that must remain an enigma wrapped inside a mystery. I can send out loving vibes and blocks of prayers, but as my wise old friend John Bunyan says, *"We delight to talk of*

the history and mystery of things, the apparent miracles, signs and wonders that suddenly jolt the heart, the delight in writings so sweetly penned.
A man may know like an angel and yet be no Christian."

"My Father is getting very old and tired, repetitive and unable to concentrate for long, incapable of taking the big decisions we need now if we are to retain our power over millions of people and before the other galaxies start revealing their hand. He doesn't understand competition. Our concept is the competition of the moral and caring forces on Earth against the negative and greedy majority so that they can provide equality of opportunity and justice that can be understood by all. We have to be able to move resources around from the rich countries to the poor but not leaving the rich countries destitute but to address the problems of disease and premature death. Cancer is a Cancer is a Cancer and we have no known cure… yet."

Many secular Jews who forswear Zionism and fundamentalism are granted transfer to the Christian Section of Heaven. We've got Einstein, Spinoza, and Kafka amongst others.

It's not only the singers but musicians, philosophers, writers and actors who are welcome and encouraged. They all add to the gaiety of the place. The residents enjoy sport facilities and plant lined arbours and walkways to gossip in.

The Heavenly Choir and Dance Group give well attended concerts. The actor's room is called Don't Look in The Mirror. Big J hasn't much time for actors and their egos.

The Muslims have a completely separate entrance to their own space which unfortunately for expectant men arriving has no welcoming virgins but plenty of grapes and cool running water spouting from spigots. When not poring over the Qur'an, they play football between themselves, though the Sunnis and Shias often clash. The Sufis just do communal dancing and yoga classes. The Saudis control the finances and are the ruling body of the football teams. Continuous fouling is punished by a leg amputation so there are a lot of one legged footballers on crutches. Players compensate with amazing facility, taking their cue from many earthly players who use their other leg to stand on, as purely decoration. A special room known as the Interim Room isolates Avicenna and Averroes from the other Muslims. Avicenna was an influential polymath of the Islamic Golden Age, a genius who wrote and studied intensively, even mastering Aristotle. He qualified as a doctor when only eighteen and said,

"Medicine is no hard and thorny science like mathematics and metaphysics."

Averroes was another extraordinary genius and also studied and wrote a medical encyclopedia. Like Avicenna he was heavily influenced by Aristotle and in his studies pursued rational explanations and causes for happenings in the world around him.

He wrote a book with my favourite title. *The Incoherence of the Incoherence.*

They are both on the Inter Faith Committee.

Their room is like sections of the London Library. There are spiral staircases up to the stacks and small desks with plenty of light flooding in from light above the rafters. Stacks and stacks of learned treatises and reference books cover the walls. Priceless instruments to study the galaxies lay on tables.

Other scholars are very welcome but not just for academic purposes.

In the middle of the room is a green table. Apart from endlessly discussing philosophical and metaphysical subjects, the two great minds share a consuming passion. Table Tennis. Every moment away from studying is spent pushing, smashing, chopping, and spinning little white balls across a net.

Avicenna told me that when he and Averroes first started playing it was very simple.

"A sort of Ping Pong" I suggested.

There were intakes of breath and a horrified look on their faces.

"Ping Pong !!!"

Avicenna said "My esteemed friend. Please never call what we play Ping Pong.

We were skilled and resourceful, used wooden bats and concentrated on seeking out the weakness of the opponent."

"We played long rallies and thought about our tactics," said Averroes

A tall man with flowing golden locks and wearing an elegant frock coat, breeches and polished black leather boots and another man in a suit and carrying an umbrella came into the room.

The man in a three piece suit had bushy eyebrows and was wearing glasses.

"Let me introduce Sir Isaac Newton and Sir Isaiah Berlin" said Avicenna.

"They have been the source of endless changes in the nature of our games"

Sir Isaiah laughed. "All we did was to try and modernize these two."

Sir Isaac joined in "Yes we got them to think about the thickness or thinness of the sponge, its hardness which plays an important factor on the speed of table tennis rubber. Thickness, hardness, density are needed we drummed into them."

Averroes was becoming very animated "Both of us believed the advent of so much sophisticated equipment had an adverse dramatic effect on the game.

We have agreed to differ."

"So come. Let us to battle" declaimed Sir Isaac.

I watched fascinated as these intellectual giants played ferociously for an hour and a half, behaving I am glad to say with impeccable manners. Sir Isaac's height enabled him to leap high in the air before delivering his favourite shot, a round arm smash that invariably missed the table edge. Sir Isaiah was a much more circumspect player, taking few risks but made consistent and looping returns. He had to stop frequently to wipe the mist fogging up his glasses.

The main problem for them as partners was that both are left handed.

Sir Isaac's backhand often disturbed Sir Isaiah's forehand but they muddled through. The two Islamic scholars were very amusing, taking lots of little breaks to discuss tactics with hands across their mouths. Both were excellent spin players and relished the chop shot. They also loved playing way back from the table sending persistent returns just over the net.

I left them wiping the sweat from their faces with striped towels.

All were in good humour and already turning towards their respective desks and piles of books.

In Christian Heaven, Thomas Hobbes is Head of The Referees.

His dictum that if man didn't submit to a ruler or ruling body *"life would be nasty, poore, brutish and short"*, concentrates offender's minds, given Thomas has the power to recommend a life sentence to the nether regions.

Big J's Father is becoming an increasingly remote figure, out of touch with not only The Earth but the other Galaxies. His is still the Final Word with the Holy Dove flitting about, taking soundings from the great and the good before settling on his shoulder and whispering advice in his ear. It has been noticed that these days The Holy Dove often settles on Big J's shoulder and whispers in his ear.

The Angels look concerned and whisper amongst themselves.

The Big Decision which is forever being debated is when to let the Earth People know there are other peoples, other Galaxies, other faiths but He is reluctant to disturb the status quo, though one day He will have to come clean.

Big J retains a discreet presence, sensitive to the different sects and apparently content to see the Buddhists arrive and disappear in a puff of smoke.

The Hindus come and reappear in different guises, flit between Galaxies but they are no problem usually. He gets a little cross with us agnostics. "Wobblies" he calls us. He has led a charmed life since his crucifixion and has only the scars to show now. Mary is besotted with him and the brothers and sisters get very little attention, especially his brother James. I have never seen Joseph. Mary is of course Queen of Heaven and a charming lady, ready to chat about her history. I had always been curious about her House in Italy. Her version basically followed the story line passed down through the centuries, though she did have a naughty twinkle in her eyes as she related her account. On May 10 1291, the shepherds of Tersatto, in former Yugoslavia woke up and were surprised to find a house had appeared on the plain where they kept their sheep. They woke up the village Priest, Father Alexander who fearfully entered the house.

He found an ancient altar and a statue of Mary. She told me it was quite a good likeness. The building became an object of veneration until one night it disappeared. Apparently a band of guerrilla angels led by St Michael had lifted it and taken it on a journey to various sites. Finally they settled it down on a hill near Loreto in the Marche, Italy. She recalled revealing herself to a saintly hermit in 1296, (she is always very precise about dates) and identifying her former, now somewhat transformed home. She still grants the occasional cure to afflicted souls. Mary agrees that no reports ever came out of the Middle East of the disappearance of a house from the backstreets of Nazareth.

"Can you imagine the headlines?"

"The Bar Joseph house, just off the Via Immaculata, former home of Mary the mother of former Guerrilla leader Jesus bar Joseph disappeared last night. The authorities are investigating the matter."

She laughed when I said,

"I thought perhaps you hadn't paid the rent and done a moonlight."

"Moonlight?"

You know, had it away on your toes, legged it, done a runner" I said in mock cockney.

"Your parents were Cockneys?"

"Stand on me, would I tell any porkies, they were both born wivin sound of Bow Bells. Me Dad in Silvertown, the old lady in Hackney."

More than fifty Popes have issued bulls testifying to the authenticity of the Loreto House. I asked Virgin Mary about the many sightings of her throughout the years since her Assumption, when she was hoisted up to Heaven by her Girdle and given a sumptuous Coronation. I asked her particularly about Knock in Ireland where she made an appearance in 1879. A Monsignor James Haran led a campaign to build an airport on the site. "Well I am particularly fond of that place as I am, appropriately enough the Patron Saint of Pilots." The airport was opened in 1986. I asked her which her favourite title was; "Our Lady of Mercy," "Our Lady of Joy," "Our Lady of Sorrows" maybe?

Or what about Our Lady of The Snow?

She thought about it for a minute;

"Yes I love that name and the circumstances. John was a Roman patrician and he and his wife had no children. They wanted to leave their possessions to me and were looking for a sign. On a hot August evening at the height of the Roman summer, snow fell on the Esquiline Hills. I don't know if anyone here had anything to do with it" she said archly. "John took it as the sign he had been waiting for and he and his wife had the church of Santa Maria Maggiore built. Every year a bagful of white petals is shaken free high up inside the nave and drifts gracefully to the floor to commemorate the event"

"So that's your favourite…"

"No. Our Lady of the Fright" she said. This was a new name to me.

"When Jesus was at the start of His ministry and his fame spreading as a powerful orator throughout Judaea and Samaria, he visited the synagogue in Nazareth and felt the spirit of the Lord come upon him.

He had a magnificent and compelling voice and standing up he began to speak.

His oratory carried hypnotically into the synagogue and beyond the doors."

"He hath anointed me to preach the Gospel, to heal the brokenhearted, to preach deliverance to the imprisoned, to give sight to the blind, to set at liberty those who are bruised."

"My son's inspired words spoken with such authority and passion enraged the Elders of the Synagogue and they called out, stirring the congregation to anger. He was grabbed by the young thugs of the synagogue and dragged to the edge of Mount Precipice and they prepared to hurl him down the cliff.

I called out in fright and some of the wiser men of the synagogue called for his release and hurried him away. The church built there in 1882 was called Our Lady of the Fright in commemoration of my fear and has recently been restored."

If Our Lady has a fault it is her treatment of Diana, whom she mostly ignores.

She was taken aback at the reaction to Diana's death, shall we say a touch of the green eyed monster. I pointed out to her that Diana fulfilled a similar role to hers.

The people who mourned her revealed a deep seated residual desire for mystery, miracle and ritual. Mary remains non committal when the subject comes up.

Sometimes Big J looks so sad. He gathers us together and launches into a tirade.

"The people of the Book spend too much time on interpreting the Book when they should be loving and giving. Love manifested in action is what they should be aiming for. I've washed my hands of those Zionists who steal land

and build walls of apartheid in my birthplace. Is there any sight more obscene than bulldozers destroying olive groves, houses and murdering the young Rachel Corrie, or young children used as shields?

Is there anything crueller than suicide bombers spreading mayhem in Tel Aviv and the cities of the Earth?

I pour scorn on those Priests scrabbling around in the Church of The Holy Sepulchre in Jerusalem for donations.

Where does it say in the Bible that priests should be celibate, look what that's led to?

Did I or my Father ever say that women priests were anathema?

Who told those Ultras to wear all that gear, come rain or shine and bang their heads against a Wall? Who told their wives to wear wigs?

I've asked Mohammed time and again if he heard Gabriel properly on the subject of cruel and unusual punishments. On hatred of the Jews, on the subjugation of women, the cutting off of limbs and stoning people to death.

He says it is all later misinterpretations of the oral history handed down and interpreted in the Qu'ran by fanatics who couldn't read or spell. After all, he admits he doesn't have a perfect memory or even perfect hearing.

What words ever spoken by me or my Father condone female circumcision or the cutting off of hands, stoning or public beheadings?

How did people descend to so much depravity and arid hatreds?

When my family took over the Earth when I was a young boy from the Greeks, we had such high hopes for the future. Vitruvius had drawn up a master plan for a new home for the Greek Gods, and a New Earth project. The negotiations took place on Mount Olympus and had been interminable. Zeus, Poseidon and Hades were all very imposing figures, with flowing beards and masses of curly hair. They claimed the sky, sea and the underworld, saying the Earth was common to all. We put forward our plans showing our new Earth. Too much mayhem and blood was associated with the old Earth; all that killing and incestuous begatting in the Old Testament.

My Father agreed it had to go. He confessed to me later he had never really recovered from the effort of creating the new Earth.

"I rested on the seventh day and said to myself, "I hope it works, with my fingers crossed behind my back." We worked together on a formula to ease out Zeus and the old guard. We agreed they could keep the sky and the sea. That was my biggest mistake. People pray to me to interfere in the floods, the tsunamis, the oil spills, destruction of the fish and fauna of the sea bed. But I can do nothing. Remember Zeus, Poseidon and Hades shook lots in a golden helmet for control of the sky, sea and underworld. Zeus took the Skies, Hades the Underworld and Poseidon the Seas.

We have tried to renegotiate the treaty but we always come up against Zeus's family.

So many wives and children. I don't think you people realize the monsters he created. His brother Poseidon is a surly quarrelsome sort and mopes around his underwater palace hitting servants with his trident at the merest misdemeanour.

The white chariot horses who draw his golden chariot can at his behest quell storms and tempests but he has to be in the mood.

Does any one read Greek mythology anymore?

You love gardening Ricky but would you want to let loose Priapus in your garden?

He is an ugly child with enormous genitals and goes nowhere without his pruning knife. He's a sadist and killer."

"The Greeks gave us the Olympics?" I said.

"Ah, in those days they were an event of joy. Hostilities between countries ceased whilst they took place. I heard tales as a young man of the glories of the pentathlon.

But those stories pale in comparison with Jim Thorpe."

"Jim Thorpe?"

"Burt, come and tell Ricky about Jim."

Burt Lancaster, as ever all teeth and sinister smile came over, his splayed feet and gliding walk betraying his circus acrobat background.

"Hi Ricky, how you doing?

Jim Thorpe was the greatest all round sportsman ever. He was never recognized as such because he was a Native American. His people weren't even granted citizenship until 1924. Can you believe that? In his own country? He's over there practicing his touch downs with the American team.
It's hard to know where to start with Jim's story."

Big J said, "He was born to a Catholic mixed race couple of the Sac and Fox tribe.

His native name was, "Path lit by flash of lightening "

"I called him Bright Path," said Burt.

"How did you meet him?"

Burt looked cross. "You didn't see *Man of Bronze?*"

"I'm afraid not."

"I played Jim. He was in the film too"

"In long shot I think Burt" said Big J crisply.

"The film starts out with me walking past this group of high school sports jocks practising the high jump. I'm in my street clothes and ask them if I can have a go.

"Be our guest" sniggers one of the guys.

"I jump five foot nine inches, out of sight of any of them."

Big J interrupted him. "Jim was a phenomenon. So good at all field sports he made the 1912 Olympic team for the pentathlon and decathlon and won both Gold Medals

He played top class football, basket ball, baseball"

"They took the medals away from him because he had been paid to play semi professional basketball at one time."

Big J and Burt were getting so excited, competing to tell the story.

"He got them back thirty years after his death after a review by the IOC"

"When did he get here?

Burt looked at Big J.

"1953. He had gone downhill during the Great Depression.

Played Indian chiefs in some bad movies, He drank too much.

He could never escape the racial profiling. When he scored the winning points for Carlisle College against an Army team the Wall Street Journal headline was

"Indians scalp Army."

Big J sighed "What have the Olympics become?

They've been corrupted by boycotts, bribery, doping and terrorism."

"So where are all the Gods now?" I asked

"Zeus was offered a home with us, but he and his fellow Gods decided to retire to their own planet above Mount Olympus."

"What about the Underworld?"

"We agreed on a joint occupation."

"What about the Buddha and all the Hindu deities?"

"They are always a law unto themselves in their own Haven.

Enigmatic personages but we are never quite sure where they spend the bulk of their time. I often wish more of them would help. When I asked The Buddha once, he replied,

"It is yours to swelter at the task."

"A bit Pontius Pilate don't you think? you can't wash your hands of everything.

Old Gandhi is always willing to help

He says the old dishonoured policies were to be replaced by universal messages of love and peace. Yet we have spent all these years struggling to burn that message into the people's souls only to arrive at an arrogant and narrow interpretation of what it means to be a human being. Too many people frittering their lives away immersed in guilt and recrimination, in negativity and cruelty.

Why did I personally oversee The Enlightenment?

To end up with bigots, charlatans and knaves?

A brief window of opportunity was lost.

The Holy Books are not Holy Writ. They are parables to be discussed.

But please not endlessly. Too many bible bashers spend too much time on interpretation instead of good works. All these insular and frantic Movements that proliferate daily; Evangelicals, Charismatic Christians, Speaking in Tongues, Television Evangelists. They are all inherently schismatic and end up being about the love of power rather than the power of love. It leads to anti-intellectualism,

"I'll become a cabbage for my Guru" mentality.

My good and trustworthy adviser the Marquis de Montaigne wisely observes;

"That most things are unknowable but one subject about whom a man might discover something is himself. It is not enough to recount experiences.

They must be weighed and sorted, digested and distilled so that they may yield the searchings and conclusions they contain.

We spend too much time concerned about dying and forget how to live."

"I would that your leaders had imbibed his philosophies.

I have to endure prayers and pleadings wafting up here from the likes of Blair and Bush."

"You are my personal saviour and I am reborn" they bleat in their tinny, baby voices and juvenile prose as they send thousands to their deaths.

Reborn? I've got news for them.

The mass murderer Richard Milhouse Nixon has long gone below.

And so will Kissinger when his time comes.

We had thunder, lightening and demonstrations all day up here when they announced his Nobel Peace prize.

A pox on all their houses.

Our major problem today is the United States of America.

A new Imperial power always comes along to upset any progress towards a fairer Earth. Americans just won't grow up and continue to live in some mythical land of the Free. "All men are created equal." Jefferson knew that was a lie.

Surrounded by slaves and Native Americans, the American people subjugated the blacks and virtually wiped out the Native Americans.

A series of pop up presidents tried every ruse, every trick, and every delaying tactic to prevent the phrase from ever having any real meaning. George Washington believed the Native Americans could be equal but only if they were taught to live like Whites. We had hoped for some progress after the demise of the Roman and British Empires, Attila The Hun, the defeat of the Nazis, the break –up of the Soviet Union but no chance. On go the imperialist Americans. Hiroshima and Nagasaki gave them the taste of omnipotent murderous power. They followed that up with Korea and the destruction of two tiny countries, Vietnam and Cambodia. The murder and mayhem they have helped to spread in South America. Their governments spurn the democratic way, ignoring the Geneva Convention and civilized behaviour.

America has produced so much good, so many good and great people but too much wealth and hubris. The leaders trot out banalities. "This is America "We are Americans" as if to justify their existence and confer legitimacy on their destructive actions. "God Bless America" they sing.

Well He doesn't and neither do I."

They should have learnt the Native American game of Lacrosse, called the Little Brother of War. You only need one rounded object, some sticks and then attempt to hit your opponent's single post or net which can be twenty yards or a few miles away. They created the game to settle disputes rather than going to war."

Relics

I was loath to bring up the subject of relics and bided my time.

When I finally found the courage I was agreeably surprised with Big J's reaction

"Relics?"

Big J sighed. "It's a sore point between me and my Father. Over indulgence with some of the more far- fetched claims.

It all started with Helena, Constantine's mother.

She had built two of the most famous Christian shrines in the world, The Church of my birth in Bethlehem and of my death in Jerusalem, The Church of the Holy Sepulchre.

She's a lovely lady and has been here a long time. She is on very close terms with my Father.

Where do you want to start?"

"The Stairs?" I said

"*Scala Santa* or *Holy Staircase?*" said Big J raising his eyebrows.

"There should be no problem in accepting that a flight of 28 marble steps could be and were brought back from Palestine. Equally why assume as many do, they were fake or could not have belonged to Pontius Pilate. Or that the Church Helena had built to house the Stairs, Santa Croce Gerusalemme, had its floors packed with earth from Golgotha?"

"Hold on Big J. I am not the Inquisition. I only asked."

"There lives more faith in honest doubt, believe me than in half the creeds, Tennyson tells me."

"Did CS Lewis tell you of waking up in his study in Magdalen College, feeling God's unrelenting approach *"whom I did not want to meet, that which I had greatly feared had at last come upon me. I gave in, admitted God was God, knelt and prayed."*

"I perceive hope and salvation for you Ricky.

Come on, tell me your impressions of Santa Croce."

"Well you know obviously that the steps are now encased in wood out of piety.

After all your Holy Feet used them and your blood stains the steps.

I climbed them because I wanted to see if I felt sin dropping away from me and a reason might be revealed to persuade me to want to be welcomed into your Kingdom. I reached the top feeling exultant."

"You'll always be welcome here if we all survive the tests to come." Big J smiled,

"You know the more steps you climb the bigger the indulgence. Poor old Martin Luther who fancied himself an athlete had to give up half way and he was only about twenty five years old. I note handrails have recently been installed to aid the faithful the curious and the obese."

"What of the Chapel full of relics? Not just one but two thorns from The Crown of Thorns, and splinters from the True Cross?"

"Why not? You don't deny I was crucified and nailed on a wooden cross?

"No, I just have a few problems with the survival of your crib from the stable at Bethlehem, Doubting Thomas's mummified finger, the very one he poked in your side to test that Longinus had really pierced your side with his spear…" I hesitated.

"Go on. There are no Papal edicts against discussion here"

"I find it very difficult"

"Unlike you to not say what you think."

"The Holy Foreskin," I blurted out.

"Ah… which one, the one in Bomarzo or the one in Abruzzi?

Look I plead guilty to not accepting they are my collective foreskins or that Veronica wiped away my sweat with her veil. I can't always give definitive answers.

You will understand why one day.

I would like to end this very interesting discourse with CS Lewis again.

"I believe in Christianity as I believe that the sun has risen. Not only because I see it but because by it I see everything else."

Earth in All Its Majesty

I enjoy my heaven trips and now finally I have learnt some of the truths of The Father and The Son and their acceptance and revelations on the existence of other Galaxies, it all starts to make sense. I have accepted that certain questions must be left unasked, certain people not inquired after. Big J will only go part of the way in explaining the deeper mysteries of life. He says there are unchartered acres to fill in where we can dig for tranquility on our own allotments. I believe that nothing will be resolved until all the galaxies agree to a final conference. Big J says that one of man's besetting sins is to create committees, sub committees and inquiries that lead to endless debate whilst people starve and their minds remain empty of thought and energy.

The Scottish Enlightenment philosopher David Hume posited:

"If God is all powerful why pain?

If he is all powerful but does nothing to alleviate the pain then He is a cruel God.

If he really is powerless, then why God?"

God is none of those things. He and Big J are special and unique but essentially powerless until the Galaxies join together to create another New Earth.

The questions the scientists want to ask are the same questions Big J and his teams are asking.

What happened before the big bang?

Big J knows that primordial chaos was not moulded into a single universe by someone called God. Every day they are witnesses to actions from other planets and look down on their own creation with fear and wonder. Will science and scientists discover new ways for the Earth to develop?

In a way Big J and his teams are in competition with Earth. They recognize the need to control the seismic increase in the Earth's population. The human right to reproduce is unsustainable. The earthlings can recycle, renew energy resources, produce more food but each new baby adds to the problem.

What of us oldies? Living longer even if that means a forlorn figure alone in a chair in some forsaken nursing home; unable to feed or relieve ourselves or recognize our visitors. Who is going to pay for our incarceration in overheated institutions smelling of carbolic, decay and decrepitude, where eyes that can no longer see ask the same questions

"Was I there?,"

"Are we there yet?"

"Where's my dinner?"

"Bed pan! Bed pan!"

The computer geniuses claim a new technology called a 3D printer might be the saviour of mankind. One takes a design from the computer and makes it into a physical object. Press "Print" and out comes a "thing." Like what?

A pen, a phone, an implant. Please don't take my word for it.

I read it in the Guardian so it must be true.

I know that man is held responsible for the evils of the world and most people give God the credit for the good things. I am not sure I think that is a fair bargain.

Tonight in my garden I watched butterflies flitting from shrub to shrub, a spider agonisingly spinning its web and joy of joys, a young song thrush, its speckled front only just developing appear about three feet from my chair and as if I didn't exist, proceeded to bash a snail's shell on the paving stones, finally dragging out his meaty prey. On such nights fortified by the gleam of the evening sun and a bottle of wine, I bend the knee and acknowledge the wonder of the gods.

Sometimes people are tempted by Pascal. If you believe, he wrote, you have nothing to lose. When you reach the "pearly" gates; bingo.

If you don't believe, Disaster descends as Peter turns you away.

The World Cup 2010

Big J convened an English Football Sports Forum at the request of the old international players. All the players were in football shorts and jerseys. They wore their international caps, those schoolboy-like caps with tassels hanging down.

He chaired the discussion.

"Let's have a brief introduction from Bobby on the World Cup in general and then move on to the perennial problem of England's dismal displays in World Cups."

Bobby stood up, his blond hair gleaming, his open and honest face shining.

"We have just witnessed one of the crudest, nastiest, arid World Cup Finals in FIFA's history. All the Dutch cared about was winning. To obtain their dream of a World Cup triumph they set out to stifle, intimidate and injure one of the best teams of modern times, the Spanish.

The Dutch defenders fouled, fouled again and still hadn't finished.

Don't listen to me, listen to what Johan Cruyff, who was the epitome of total football said about his own country's performance;"

"Regrettably sadly they played very dirty... this ugly, vulgar hard hermetic hardly eye catching hardly football style, yes it served the Dutch to unsettle Spain. If with this they got satisfaction fine, but they ended up losing. They were playing anti-football."

"Bless Johan's honesty"

"Johnny Haynes?" said Big J

One of the greatest passer's of a ball in modern times stood up.

I had played with Haynes in a London Representative game when we were teenagers.

"Good to see Ricky here. Still got all your hair I see. Well me old mates, Spain have developed a sublime passing game where each player produces passes that are telepathic. I have suffered so much watching England where the player's thought processes can be seen when they receive the ball.

The thoughts amount to, "What do I do now, whom shall I pass to? Shall I whack it downfield? Oh Don Fabio will get mad so I think… oh no someone's nicked the ball off me."

Tommy Lawton interrupted politely.

"The Spanish have one fault. They have no deadly strikers able to break the deadlock put on them by some teams. David Villa never stops working and scores great goals, Torres on form, is fast and brilliant, but they need someone who can mix it and get amongst the defenders."

Wilf Mannion came in excitedly "Iniesta was one of my favourites of the tournament. The patterns the Spanish weave are hypnotic but can lull one to sleep."

Two men stood up at the same time. The taller of them had only one leg.

"After you Arthur"

"Well I did score more goals than you."

Big J, always good on statistics said;

"But you played a lot more games Arthur."

We were in the presence of two of the greatest goal scorers of all time.

The man who had had his right leg amputated was Dixie Dean whose statue outside Everton's Goodison Park is a testament to his status. In 1926 he fractured his skull and jaw in a motor accident. Doctors feared he wouldn't play again.

His first goal back in the side was a header.

In the 1927-1928 season he scored one hundred goals, sixty of them in the League, still a record.

Arthur Rowley I saw at Fulham in 1949, where he scored nineteen goals in twenty two games. He moved onto Shrewsbury. His career total was four hundred and thirty four goals.

"Yes, they need a ruthless striker, someone who might stand back a little from the intricate passing patterns going on around him. A robust, fearless, dare I say old fashioned centre forward."

He paused for effect "Like Dixie."

"Or Arthur" said Dixie.

"Anybody got any other recommendations?", asked Big J.

A discreet cough drew our attention to a handsome man with a wonderful head of hair. A murmur went round the room "Just Fontaine."

Big J laughed "How could we not mention you Just, 30 goals in 21 games for France. You were a blur of speed, ball control and sheer verve when you scored thirteen goals in the 1958 World Cup."

"What of Ferenc Puskas?", growled the iconic Hungarian player

"When you were a bit, shall we say a little slimmer Ferenc" said Stanley Matthews.

A roar of laughter went up as we looked at the popular roly poly figure of Ferenc and his mischievous face.

1953 was etched on my memory but so was the 1960 European Cup Final.

I watched Ferenc on television destroy Eintracht with four goals, the equally sublime Di Stefano scoring three.

Not a centre forward in the sense I am thinking of but the greatest poacher of goals I ever saw and played against was Jimmy Greaves.

Don Capello

We had a break for coffee and angel cakes and I chatted with Johnny about the old days. When we sat down again Big J said, "Okay let's talk about Don Fabio.

Who wants to start?"

Danny Blanchflower put his hand up. "The English never seem to get it right. You pay this guy millions of pounds because he has a good track record.

He starts off giving the impression of being tough, uncompromising and good at man management. He then proceeds to prove the opposite. Having vowed no player who wasn't one hundred per cent fit would be considered or whose current form was wavering, what happens?

Ledly King, as close to a crippled footballer as you can get is selected.

Ledly can't train after one game in the Premier League. What does his selection tell the young hopefuls out there? Rio Ferdinand had played a handful of matches, has a serious and recurring back problem. Barry is not fit but the Don will wait on him. James Carragher is long past his best and Upson has not had a good season.

Fabio even was considering waiting for Owen Hargreaves who hasn't played for nearly two years. Fabio gets his assistant Baldini to telephone the thirty five year old Paul Scholes asking him to join the party with two days to go."

Big J stopped Danny in full flow. He was always famous for his monologues as well as his football skills. Big J pointed to Frank Swift.

"Frank?"

"Frying Pan Hands" as he was nicknamed, smiled. He waved his massive hands around as he spoke. "The goal keeping situation was the most stupid and farcical of the Capo Di Capo's decisions. David James had been injured for weeks, Green naturally thought after playing so many matches he would be first choice. Joe Hart should have been first choice. He's a talented young man for now and the future.

We need to get back to having a regular goalkeeper who everybody trusts to give confidence to the defenders."

There was a respectful silence as Frank sank back into his chair and Duncan Edwards stood up. Built like an oak tree trunk, both Duncan and Frank had been killed in the Munich plane crash that wiped out a generation of footballers.

"Lampard and Gerrard were again the dilemma twins. They play as if in a deep maze unaware where each other are. They galvanise themselves into frenetic activity every now and then only to quickly sink back into a deadly torpor.

James Milner is too slow and unimaginative to ever be a world class player.

Lennon is like a greyhound out of the trap in open field.

"Run Rabbit Run Rabbit run run run"

He never catches the Rabbit and if he did he wouldn't know whether to grill it or eat it raw." Stan Mortenson stood up. He had been a chunky bustling forward for Blackpool and England.

He was the only survivor from a plane crash when he was serving in the RAF.

The people of Blackpool raised money for a statue of him at Bloomfield Road and a stand is named after him. He is the only player to have scored a hat trick in an FA Cup Final at Wembley, the famous game in which Blackpool, inspired by Morty's goals and Stanley Matthews' wing wizardry came back from 3-1 down to win 4-3.

"I don't think Defoe is ever going to be a top international performer, nor is Crouch. Heskey was a decent front man but froze if presented with a shot on goal.

Wayne Rooney? Never in the field of World Cup football have I been so gutted, so sick at heart that an English player's talent had deteriorated so far.

I hope and pray he will recover, because he is a great talent."

There was a murmur of agreement around the table but Nat Lofthouse banged the table earning a sharp glance from Big J.

"I agree he is a talented lad but the first mistake Cappello made was to join in the chorus that he was our key player and without him our chances would be slim.

Where have we heard that before? A certain Mr Beckham?

Spain managed to reach and win the Final without any major contribution from Torres. Rooney has never delivered for England when it has mattered.

Sent off in a previous World Cup, he has not changed a course of a match or thrilled us as spectators. Why did the Great Disciplinarian not substitute him except in one game? Rooney was surly, miserable and couldn't control simple passes first time or send any decent shots towards goal. I don't like being so hard on him but he is I am afraid on a downward spiral. Ferguson says "Wait until 2014, the lad was tired, overworked, weighed down by the expectation."

I can't take any more of these clichés."

With the authority of a World Cup winner Sir Alf Ramsey spoke up.

"Neither can I Nat. Ashley Cole and Johnson looked mediocre compared to Phillip Lahm or Ramos or most of the other full backs on display. None of them could put a candle to my 1966 full backs George Cohen and Ray Wilson. I see Real Madrid is expressing an interest for Cole at £30 million; truly mad.

"Absolutely Sir Alf" said Bobby Moore.

"I can't take Terry or Gerrard any more telling us "we know what's to be done and we're going out there to do it."

Big J was about to bring the session to a close.

"Enough already gentleman. All of them should retire from international football.

Let us give thanks that Fabio has gone.

I would sack the lot and start with new players from the under twenty ones.

Get 'Arry, keep Pearcy and bring in Hope Powell."

We all applauded.

Part Six

"But no man may deliver his brother nor make agreement unto God for him."
Book of Common Prayer Psalm 49

What Happened To Us?

All older people say they don't know where the years have gone. We joke about bits and pieces falling off our bodies, of forgetting where our spectacles are, of repeating ourselves. We say it never happened in our day and that manners have got worse and young people don't appreciate the sacrifices former generations made for them.

I don't know. I know I don't like people cycling on the pavement, or playing loud music on the Tube or gobbing on the pavement.

I have a big problem with burquas.

It is irrational on one level I know and makes me appear intolerant. Let me try to explain. I read once that in some societies in Africa, the village elders call a halt to proceedings under the banyan tree when it gets dark. The rationale is that it is impossible to argue in the dark. Why?

Because to pursue an argument requires being able to see your opponent's face to determine whether the words are matching what the eyes are saying. I agree with that. The most ridiculous situations have come about because some Muslims insist on their right to wear full covering of the face. A media lecturer, a Teaching Assistant in a primary school are two examples. How can you communicate with small children of all backgrounds from behind the veil? How can a media lecturer of all people teach that part of the course dealing with communication and interviewing, without using her own communication skills in debate in full view of her students?

Muslim teaching enjoins Muslims living in countries where the faith is not in a majority to obey and act according to the law and mores of the country they live in, as long as their religion isn't insulted. It is I think insulting for some Muslims to insist on full veiling. We the infidels will want their women is the inference.

Is it okay for Saudi Princes to engage foreign prostitutes whilst protecting and veiling their own ladies? The western community with all its faults gains much of its attractions because of its openness. The shaking of hands and looking into people's faces is a part of the social cement that keeps us tolerant and civilized to each other.

From the point of view of sport, the veil isolates Muslim women from their contemporaries of other faiths or none. Could a veiled Muslim woman swim, pole vault, throw discuss, play football or cricket in open competition?

An unveiled Muslim Moroccan woman named Nawal El Moutawakel was the first Muslim female born in Africa to win a Gold Olympic Medal. She won the 400 metres hurdles in Los Angles in 1984 after being trained at the Iowa State University. The King of Morocco ruled that all girls born on the day of her victory would take her first name.

It is not freedom but isolation that the veil demands.

I like queues and politeness and respect for older people, respect for all our fellow citizens.

I don't like arrogant yobs from the City, braying in the wine bars and despising the "working class." I don't like building sites full of strutting overweight men in yellow hats and great boots who are convinced that all women fancy them. I intensely dislike spoilt and rude children, especially on the London Tube sprawling all over the seats and ignoring the elderly without a seat. I definitely don't like mobiles in the theatre and cinema, the constant anxious perusing of text messages and people walking blindly across the road or shopping areas talking on their phones.

It's like a monotonous twenty four hour fear of missing a message which will probably be about "what time are we meeting in the pub?".

But more deeply I care about the speed and greed of modern life, the lack of respect for creating something of value, of people not recognising the beauty of the environment and thus contributing to its demise.

Making something today has been downgraded to a product spewed out of a machine not a process of skill and attention to detail. Learning a craft was once synonymous with young boys of fifteen working for seven years as an apprentice.

They learnt how to use lathes, lay bricks, turn wood, fit boilers and smelt iron, make ingots.

My world in 1945 and through the fifties had as a given the industrial world of skills which had been hard earned and proudly trumpeted.

As this world shrank and the long industrial revolution finally ground to a lame ending, the workers panicked and lost their way.

The trade unions forged in unity and a strong belief in their fellow workers became reactionary forces. We had come a long way from The Tolpuddle Martyrs and Joseph Arch and the Agricultural Union. The ruling class's greed and desire to hold onto power created factions and a deep seated and heartfelt anger, especially amongst those who had spent five or six years in uniform "fighting for King and Country."

The once proud dockers marched against black immigrants.

The year England won the World Cup in 1966, *The Guardian* reported that "The colour bar at Euston Station ended yesterday." Barbara Castle announced in Parliament that British Railways, after negotiations with The National Union of Railwaymen, that no grade would in future be closed to coloured workers. Mr Asquith Xavier had taken on the railwaymen and won.

The Standing Conference of West Indian Organizations whilst welcoming the ruling remained sceptical whether it really meant the end of every type of colour prejudice in British Rail. Later under Thatcherism the mighty Miners Unions were bludgeoned into submission, their communities destroyed and their leadership losing their focus. The streets and the valleys, the waste grounds still empty after the bombing of World War Two no longer had three stumps chalked on a fence or an outline of a goal.

In the fifties budding footballers still played in the streets with tennis balls and jackets as improvised goals. A real football was usually in the ownership of some stuck up kid whom we had to suck up to if we wanted to borrow the prize. The child who had an adaptor was the most popular kid on the estate, as the air filled the bladder, a rising sense of joy and excitement filled the smelly housing estate stairwell.

When we graduated to playing in the park with real goal posts we had to pay extra for nets. Now the children who live next door to me have a real miniature goal with nets, and parade in authentic Chelsea kits costing a small fortune.

Kids never play in the street or go to the parks. "Too many perverts" says Mum.

The street as an artery of life is reduced to a highway for cars. So there are no dirty knees or flushed and ruddy faces, no bleeding football scars from the hard pavements, no scuffed shoes or torn trousers, no friendships across class lines or disputes settled with fists not knives. Fathers and Soccer Mums at School and club games scream abuse at referees and the opposition, their contorted faces conveying hatred of the Other. Their obese offspring, girls and boys crowd around the referee disputing his or her decisions, aping the banal antics of their professional heroes.

I once fought a battle in Greenwich Park with Dave Somerville, a boy from a local well known boxing family. He was a good looking boy with a broken nose.

He thought I was trying to show off my imagined superior intellect and being grand because of our big house as we played on the swings and challenged me to a fight.

Of course we fought to Queensbury rules. We hadn't been corrupted by Television and American violence in films.

At our boxing clubs we learnt combination punches, jabs, protective clinches and respect for your opponent. No kicking or wrestling but fists held high and circling each other, feinting and jabbing, looking for an opening. My mother pulled us apart which was a relief as I was getting a pasting. She took us into the house, stuck us in the bath together where we looked shamefacedly at each other, silently soaping and rubbing the blood off our faces with flannels. Mum found an old shirt of my Father's and gave it to Dave. She ruffled his hair and said,

"These trousers will fit you and what about this pullover?"

Dave was a proud lad, hesitated and looked at me.

"See if they fit you. You've got bigger muscles than my Dad."

That did it. He put them on and they were perfect.

We slicked back our wet hair like Bruce Woodcock's and sat at the kitchen table.

Mum gave us lemonade, broken biscuits and rock cakes and told her favourite joke.

"A man is called George Stinks. He hated the name and decided to change it. He went home and announced proudly he had a new name."

"What is it?"

"Bill Stinks."

It isn't very funny but because my mother enjoyed it so much and could hardly tell it for laughing, we all collapsed in laughter.

Mum made us shake hands before we parted and throughout the rest of our youth we looked out for each other and were great friends whenever we met.

Craftsmanship

Craftsmanship is forging something out of raw material whether as an object or an ideal. Today's superstars take the field in sponsored shirts, shorts, boots and headbands. Hairstyles are carefully chosen and tattoos emphasise trendiness and masculinity. The look supersedes the performance. Product is winning at any cost, winning ugly not a cry of shame but necessity. If we can't grasp the process because it's too complicated, too complex, we dismiss it and cut to the chase to obtain the desired product.

I know it's not just football. It goes through all our culture. Anti-elitism has taken deep roots. To show your knowledge is a faux pas as are high culture references. These cultural tags are too universal, too human, an affront to badges and manifestoes. We live in a mismatch of realities, a tapestry of expectation in every day life.

Jake and Dinos Chapman do not carve or model their figures by graft, sweat and bodily exertion with their hands. Rachel Whitread does not sculpt her work but takes casts. Gilbert and George followed by the word Artists is an oxymoron.

They photograph their subjects whether it is pretty boys or their own shit and put the results in carefully designed factory-made metal frames. They are con artists of genius, poseurs who bludgeoned any criticism of their puerile talents into the dust.

Race and Prejudice

"I look to a day when people will not be judged by the color of their skin but by the content of their character."
Martin Luther King

Growing up in South London in the forties and fifties it was rare to see a black or brown face. At primary school we were all white. Black people were referred to as nig nogs. At Grammar School five boys out of several hundred used to march in after the hymns and prayers and stand silently isolated at the front whilst school business was given out by the Headmaster. They were Jewish and bore no resemblance in my mind to the people my father referred to as Yids and as played by Alec Guinness in *Oliver Twist*. They certainly did not look like the emaciated and piled up bodies from Belsen that we had seen on Pathe News. Despite the horror of the Holocaust, I grew up hearing about Jews who had lots of money and were not to be trusted and blacks who were inferior. My mother's hero Winston Churchill referred to the noble Gandhi as the naked fakir. When Gandhi went to visit King George VI at Buckingham Palace the King said

"you are wearing very few clothes Mr. Gandhi."
He replied,
"You are wearing enough for us both, Your Majesty."
We learnt a filtered history in which despite a lot of evidence to the contrary, Britain was the land of hope and glory, the owners still of vast tracts of foreign fields and lots of little black and brown people who loved us.

Black men had won the World Heavy Championship in America and we all knew about The Brown Bomber Joe Louis.

He was okay because he had beaten Max Schmelling who was a Nazi.

It was years later that I learnt the truth about Max, a brave man who helped Jews and later befriended the broken and bankrupt Louis and raised funds for him.

I was fortunate to meet Blessing and her mother.

I was once trying to articulate my mother's attitude to them both.

"You see Sheila, my mother says that she's not prejudiced but it's the children of mixed couples who suffer."

Sheila gave me her wise smile.

"They only suffer if you are prejudiced. My daughter is a beautiful product of two races, two human beings. She's half black and half white, half mine and half her father's but she is my Blessing and a human being in her own right. I and she don't have to defend, justify or apologise to any one." To her credit my mother countered my Father's racism with an, albeit patronizing, but fair minded attitude.

Later on she fully endorsed Sheila's words.

I had early on in my life a feeling that racism was one of the greatest evils on earth.

In our schools football team, we had a player everyone called Woggie.

I didn't know what it meant until Sheila explained and I felt ashamed of my ignorance.

What changed my attitudes forever was a musical evening with Blessing, Sheila and Edith. On every other Friday night we would sit around with hot egg sandwiches and mugs of tea whilst Edith produced from a cupboard, large, black 78rpm records in immaculate sleeves and covers. Each priceless sleeve was marked in black ink with the details of the record, the year bought and where. Sheila would tell us about the history and back ground of each singer or piece of music. She played Josh White, an American folksinger who had achieved a big career against all the odds, becoming the first black man to play in segregated hotels. Bessie Smith was a personal favourite of mine and the story of her dying after being refused entry into a "whites only" hospital moved me deeply. As it grew dark and we were all yawning, Sheila said "Play it Edith." Sheila was very solemn.

"Children, some songs make us cry, some songs make us laugh. But very few songs change history. Leonard Feather, a famous jazz writer wrote about this song that it was, "the first significant protest in words and music; the first unmuted cry against racism."

It was written by a Jewish man called Abe Meeropol who said,

"I wrote Strange Fruit because I hated lynching and I hate injustice and I hate the people who perpetuate it."

"What's lynching?", asked Blessing

Edith drew out of the cover a double photograph and passed it to Blessing.

She drew back in horror as she looked at the picture and beckoned me over.

A black man was tied by the throat to the back fender of a car being dragged through the streets. The second picture showed him burnt and hung up from a tree with insolent white men in panamas and smoking cigars leaning nonchantly against the trees, grinning and laughing. "People would send postcards of pictures like this to relatives boasting, "this is what happens to uppity niggers." Sheila continued,

"An extraordinary singer made this her personal hymn. She was Billie Holiday who sadly, scarred by racism and her addiction to drink and drugs died aged forty four.

That's her on the cover. She always sung with a white gardenia in her hair. Lester Young a great saxophone player and her good friend nicknamed her "Lady Day."

I heard her sing this song at the Albert Hall in 1954 and have never forgotten its impact on me and my life.

I am going to read the lyrics to you before we listen."

"Southern trees bear a strange fruit
Blood on the leaves and blood at the root
Black body swinging in the Southern breeze,
Strange fruit hanging from the poplar trees

Pastoral scene of the gallant South
The bulging eyes and the twisted mouth
Scent of magnolia sweet and fresh
And the sudden smell of burning flesh

Here is a fruit for the crows to pluck
For the rain to gather, for the wind to suck
For the sun to rot, for a tree to drop
Here is a strange and bitter crop"

Edith reverently placed the record on the turntable.
We sat in the gloom and listened intently to the husky, smoky voice curling through the room, laden and laced, it seemed, with centuries of hatred and sadness.

Billie finished. Blessing drew a sobbing breath.

Sheila, Edith and I had tears streaming down our cheeks.

We sat for about ten minutes in silence.

I quietly got up and went home.

I was in for further shocks as I uncovered through Sheila's library the racism of the British Empire on which the sun never set. As Sheila said, "the sun never set because God would never trust the British in the dark." I was in their house one day when the door bell rang and Sheila asked me to answer it.

I opened the door to a large black man and a small pretty woman.

Sheila appeared behind me.

"Ruth my dear, how are you?

This must be Seretse. Come in, come in."

Sheila and Ruth disappeared into the lounge and I took Seretse into the garden where Blessing was practicing her forward defensive stroke. At first, for her, she was shy with Seretse but he took the bat and proceeded to hit our tennis ball bowling all over the garden. He had a booming laugh, beautiful brown eyes, and a neat moustache.

He ruffled our hair and told us he was a Chieftain in Africa but living in England he was content to become a first class cricketer and play for Surrey.

We had tea on the lawn together and he told us tales of his country, Bechuanaland.

Before they left, he said he would like us to visit him in his country one day but at the moment he couldn't go back.

"Why not?" asked Blessing

"You'll have to ask Mr Attlee that."

Sheila showed us later a newspaper with both their pictures in it and a headline

"South African Prime Minister calls marriage of Ruth Williams "disgusting."

She told us Ruth was an old friend of hers from Eltham High School.

They had served together as ambulance drivers in the WAAF during the War.

Ruth and Seretse had been refused permission to marry in an Anglican church by the Bishop of London and had instead married at Kensington Registry Office.

We met them quite often at Sheila's and he was always charming, funny and calm.

Even to our childish eyes it was easy to see how much they loved each other.

It wasn't until later I learnt how abominably the Attlee and Conservative governments had treated them. Anxious to placate the apartheid South African regime and the racist Southern Rhodesians because it was claimed, we needed their gold, a commission was set up which decreed that Seretse Khama was "eminently fit to rule his country, but for his "unfortunate marriage." It wasn't until 1963 that Seretse was restored to his rightful heritage and knighted.

Sir Seretse Khama died in Lady Ruth's arms in Gaberone in 1980.

She died in 2002 and is buried with him in the family plot at Serowe overlooking her husband's birth place.

From them and Sheila I learned that miscegenation is a thing of beauty, a word of truth, which is that we are all mixed and miscegenated, leavened by different blood lines and liaisons and that true love does conquer all.

I kept learning facts as I grew up that astonished me.

The American Army, the saviours of Europe had a segregated Army into the 1950's, despite President Truman's executive order of 1948 abolishing segregation.

A black Lieutenant Colonel pilot tells of returning from battle and two years in a German Prison Camp where, he said he had been treated as an officer and a gentleman by the Germans. As he came down the gangplank from the ship bringing the soldiers home "a little runty white corporal was standing there";

"Whites to the right, niggers to the left."

It was rare for the British army to have black officers throughout World War II.

Black people in South Africa had to use separate facilities to Whites.

Frank Worrell was the first black captain of West Indies for a full series.

When very young I played cricket for a local team, Valley Celtic on Sundays. Just to make up the numbers for all those older players. I loved the tea in thermos flasks, the cheese and pickle white bread sandwiches and the cup cakes brought along by the wives of the older players, the dappled shadows of the oak trees in Danson and Brockley Parks, the squirrels racing around tree trunks in an endless game of tag.

I gloried in chasing down a ball, hurling myself to take a catch.

That terrifying moment when I had to face my first ball.

"Middle and Leg please Umpire."

Gazing round the field as I'd seen the older players do, taking in the field positions, pretending not to hear as a menacing grizzled old trouper pawed the ground, scratching the turf with his hobnailed boots and said,

"Shouldn't you be in bed sonny?"

The sweat was pouring down my back and legs. The relief I felt if I survived the first ball as it reared past my head.

When the immigrant players from the West Indies started to play in our league, I sensed an apprehension amongst the players and their wives.
When the lads realised that here were people who had the same number of limbs as us, loved the game as much as we did, all changed.

Crass jokes that we wouldn't be able to see them as dusk descended or about the size of their penises soon gave way to tremendous tussles, no quarter given or asked and pints of beer together afterwards. Even the wives saw that there were no monsters here to be frightened of and that children have the same sense of fun, most of the time anyway.

Any one born and brought up in London in the forties and fifties will have seen tremendous changes in the ethnic mix of the capital City.
Racism and tags on people's nationalities were normal every day language.

Black people were Niggers, Darkies, Coons. Asians were Wogs. Italians were Eyeties, Japanese were Nips, Germans were Krauts, Irish were Paddies and Welsh were Taffies. Scots were Jocks and Jews were Yids.

Today some Inner London schools have more than seventy languages as the first tongue of the children. My family includes French, German, Syrian, Czech, South African, Chinese, Jews, Christians, Buddhists, Agnostics and Atheists.

Our latest recruit is a Jewish Togolese Frenchman working as a designer in Shanghai who has just become a father to his baby Moise with my French great niece, which makes me a Great Great Uncle.

A School team I coached at cricket was made up mainly of kids of Asian and Caribbean descent. The enthusiasm of the Asians was infectious.

My Captain and vice-captain would walk past me on Cricket days, grinning and saying

"Cricket today Mr. Morris."

Where are all the black cricketers of sixteen or so years ago when five black players represented England? Think of some of the names, Dean Headley, Devon Malcolm Mark Butcher, Alec Tudor, Gladstone Small, Phil de Freitas and David Lawrence.

The contrast with football is marked. Viv Anderson was the first black player to be capped for England in 1978 and Paul Ince the first to be captain.

Now at least six black players are first choice and Rio was the latest captain until his recent injuries.

And yet as I write, Luis Suarez is suspended for allegedly using racial language to Patrice Evra, the Manchester United full back. John Terry, the current England captain is to go to trial for the same offence against Rio Ferdinand's brother Anton Ferdinand, the QPR defender.

> "Bliss was it in that dawn to be alive
> But to be young was very heaven."
>
> **William Wordsworth**

Distance lends misty eyed reminiscences to us old codgers.

We use archaic language and sometimes rhyming slang if we really are in our cups. Footballers had their hair parted in the middle, had nobbly knees, were bandy legged and wore great clunky boots with massive laces. Shin pads bulged from thick socks, shorts finished demurely below the knee. The embrocation of choice was White Horse Oils, the odour penetrating the dressing room and accompanying us onto the pitch.

At Charlton many came on bikes to training, puffing on a Woodbine.

If the manager had a car, it would be an Austin Morris with plastic indicators.

Home internationals were big events. We always expected to beat Wales and Northern Ireland but Scotland was the hated enemy.

For Wembley games, thousands of kilt wearing drunken men would descend on London, especially Soho and attempt to lay it to waste, taking great delight in flashing their bare bottoms and fronts to giggling girls.

These Scots had a twisted and ignorant image of their history whether it was the kilt or the Glencoe Massacre.

Present day tourist Scotland is covered with shops and chain stores selling the "authentic" tartan to American, Canadian, Australian and English punters.

They eat scones and drink ghastly cups of tea from metal pots that spill most of the contents on the table and take home a tin of authentic shortbread.

Out of the mists of the Gorbals and small towns came some of the finest footballers to grace the pitches of the world. George Young, a right back was hewn out of rock as was the rampaging Willie Waddell and Billy Liddell for whom the phrase "bustling wingers" was invented. Billy Steel and Alex James were golden inside forwards, diminutive creators and scorers of goals. Jimmy

Cowan was a brave and fine goalkeeper. Later eye catching players included Dave Mackay, Kenny Dalglish, Denis Law and Ian St John.

The maverick amongst the treasury of talent was Jim Baxter, a doppelganger for George Best. A midfielder who took the piss out of England at Wembley when Scotland beat the World Champions in 1967 3-2 playing "keepy uppy" giving his team mates time to get into position and just for the fun of it.

He called his left foot "The Glove" and ordered trainees to go and get his "Magic Wands." He and Best could have been twins from their dark good lucks to their unique skills, inveterate womanising, drinking and gambling.

Baxter committed the unforgiveable sin against the bigots and cretins of Glasgow Rangers supporters when he made friends with some players from the Catholic Glasgow Celtic club. His lifestyle led to two liver transplants at age 55.

He lost over £200,000 in gambling and died in 2001, a wasted hulk of a man.

The King's Road Chelsea was the trendy place to hang out in the sixties, full of actors, footballers and models. I briefly had a stall in *The Chelsea Antiques Market* and met Chelsea stars, Charlie Cook and Tommy Baldwin.

Alan Hudson also became a casual drinking friend as did briefly Chelsea supporter Michael Crawford but we had a big difference of opinion on what I thought were his lack of good manners and never spoke again.

A lovely character was Fulham's left winger Tosh Chamberlain.

Quick witted and a very friendly man, he was famous with the Fulham fans for his wild crosses and misses on goal. If he got it right he broke the back of the net with the ferocity of his shot. He once took a wild swing at the ball and sent it over the riverside terracing onto a barge in the Thames. In what was probably the longest shot in football history the ball ended up seven miles down river at Brentford.

Bobby Keech was a collection of opposites. He played for Fulham at one time and we did some deals in the antique business. He was as hard to deal with in business as he was on the football field. Bobby was blond, chunky and arrogant.

At a game against Millwall at the Den a spectator yelled at him that he was "a bottle blond." Bobby had to be restrained from climbing the fence and throttling the man.

We shared a Savile Row tailor, some nights out and a lot of wine.

I liked the trips down the King's Road in his Lotus Elan. He wanted to impress people intellectually but didn't have the brain tools he needed. Bobby would read a book, pick out a few aphorisms and then trot them out at a nightclub or later in his restaurant *Football Football*. We would visit Geoffrey Bennison's shop in Pimlico and Bobby would pontificate on the objets d'art on display. Geoffrey, a plump witty queen with a face like a carved overripe cherub, indulged him and tried to guide him towards some useful books and museums. Queens fawned on him but so did the Chelsea girls of independent means. Sadly Bobby's life style caught up with him and he died of a heart attack in 1996.

George Best swaggered around in black leather jacket and black jeans posing in doorways. He came to the Market one day to buy something, "anything" he said to placate an irate girl friend. I sold him a beautiful nineteenth century orange vase decorated with Roman charioteers. The girl didn't like it and George asked me to take it back. I still have it. Over the years he held court in a Fulham Road pub, *The Queen's Elm*. Mostly inebriated he was a friendly and open man, his geniality extending as the day wore on, dispensing slurred opinions from his reserved vantage point in the pub. He had served time in Ford Open Prison and loved to talk about it with an old queen antique dealer friend of mine called Johnny Walker he had met inside. Johnny's nickname was Poof in Boots because of the fur boots he favoured, summer and winter.

The whole world knows the story of George. Not long before he died I met him at a Health Farm in Hampshire where I was trying to lose some weight. He had been given a new liver and told drinking would kill him. The Health Club had given him a free room and board for publicity purposes. I was sitting drinking a coffee when he came into the bar. The bartender immediately went to the fridge and pulled out a bottle of white wine, filled a glass and pushed it to George. He looked across at me as if he was trying to remember who I was. He held up the glass and toasted me and downed it in one long gulp. The waiter filled it again.

I was having a coffee in a bar in the King's Road when a tall leggy redhead with an Australian accent asked if the chair next to me was free. She ordered a glass of wine and asked if I would like one too. Three hours and a lot of wine later, Germaine had transformed my life. She quickly worked out my hesitation in embracing

Women's rights. Germaine Greer brutally exposed my abysmal philosophical and historical knowledge. I was overwhelmed by her and when I realised I had to go, she grabbed my hand and told me to make sure I read her book and I'd be "alright mate" said with arched eyebrows and an exaggerated Australian accent.

The Female Eunuch was indeed life changing and my relationships with women were transformed for ever. She made me think about attitudes ingrained in me by my upbringing in the fifties.

I grew up in a world where women did all the domestic work in a house, bought the food, cooked it, had the husband's dinner on the table when he came in from work, his slippers warming in front of the stove. No man I ever knew in those days changed a nappy, pushed a pram or cleaned or cooked.

I also had a rather brutish sense of my imagined sexual power. It wasn't that I lacked the courtesies but that I assumed and took the lead role in everything connected with women. Their opinions were to be listened to with a condescending smile on my face.

They waited on me, not I on them.

Women had lost their window of opportunity after the War.

Many had become highly skilled factory workers but the men took back their old roles. Most women who worked were stuffing something into bags on a dreary production line, making sandwiches or packing biscuits at Peek Freans.

The men worked at places like Siemens, and perhaps took their wives to the pub on a Saturday night. The wives would sit with other wives nursing a Rum and black or a Baby Cham whilst the men stood at the bar with pints of Brown or Pale Ale, flexing their shoulders and itching for a fight. Wives were in theory the property of their husbands and any suspected flirtation would be met with a challenge to a fight to the roving eyed one or a walloping for the wife when they got home.

An old bricklayer foreman of mine drank twelve pints on a Saturday night, eight on Sunday and his "liveners" amounted to six pints on a Monday night.

A girl who got pregnant outside of a marriage was swiftly married to the guy who even if he didn't want to marry, succumbed to threats and orders from both sides of the families involved. Some women tried to be independent but were quickly labelled tarts, whores and worse by the hypocritical mores of the times. Wages were paid in cash. Some women were trusted to hold the wage packet and dispense the various amounts, usually giving the man a couple of pounds back for his "baccy" and beer.

I was fourteen before ration books finished.

Bills were paid in cash, few people had bank accounts. Black GPO phones were slow to spread into the working class. When we finally got one, our number was Greenwich 0986. When it rang for the first time my mother picked up the receiver at arms length regarding it with suspicion and said nothing.

I persuaded her to hold it nearer and say the number.

"What Number?" "The one on the label. Greenwich 0986."

London Diversion

"Fares Please! Move right on up the bus ducky
Is that your own face dear or have you just borrowed it?
More room on top."
"Maybe it's because I'm a Londoner
That I love London Town."

I consider myself English; not for petty nationalist reasons but since the devolution of Scotland, Wales and Northern Ireland I have never felt the same about Great Britain. I prefer the name Londoner with all its connotations, a multicultural city and the glorious Technicolor nature of its inhabitants.

I feel at home, at ease and in love with London.

When I walk its hallowed grounds, I cocoon myself with the ghosts which permeate the streets and quicken the blood at every corner.

John Bunyan is buried in Bunhill Fields in a Dissenter's Grave.

He was a tinker by trade, mending household utensils and a soldier in Cromwell's Parliamentary Army between 1644 and 1647.

The word tinker became later a reference to a marginalised person which in many ways Bunyan was. He saw his personal version of God one day and spent 12 years in a dissenter's jail in Bedford and began to write a book since read by millions.

The trench fodder of the First World War carried Pilgrim's Progress in their kitbags.

It is a story of spiritual discovery in which Bunyan's hero Christian relates his journey and adventures through Vanity Fair, the Slough of Despond and The Delectable Mountains towards the Celestial City.

As a child I read and devoured the book. The wonderful invention of names like Mr Ready To Halt, Mr Valiant for Truth, Mr Standfast, Mr Feeble-Mind, Mr Pliable. My mother had an old copy illustrated with black and white engravings of the characters. Influenced by attendance at Christchurch in Greenwich High Road twice a day on Sundays and Sunday School. I would dream of falling into the Slough of Despond and waiting anxiously at The Wicket Gate.

I fought as Great-heart smiting the head off the Giant.

I was inspired and entranced by Bunyan's use of language.

"What things so pleasant that is if a man hath any delight in things that are wonderful, for instance if a man doth delight to talk of history or the mystery of things; or if a man doth love to talk of miracles, wonders or signs, where shall he find things recorded so delightful and so sweetly penned as in the holy Scripture?"

"Sweetly penned"! Who uses language like that now?

I can see his quill pen dipping into the ink and scrawling across the page as he wrote by a candle spluttering in the cold and damp cell, his eyes straining to see. He died aged sixty from a severe cold whilst at the house in Snow Hill in Holborn of his friend, a grocer.

Just opposite Bunhill Fields is the grave of another master of inspiring literature and imagery. A statue to the great evangelist John Wesley stands outside the chapel where incidentally Margaret Thatcher got married. I wonder how they would have got on.

She wouldn't have been able to handbag or browbeat him. She tried to do the opposite to his teachings, enriching the rich and antagonising the poor.

At age five Wesley had been saved from a fire at his father's rectory in Epworth, Lincolnshire. He felt, he wrote, "like a brand plucked from the fire." He had a "warm feeling" whilst walking near St Paul's Cathedral and went on to preach open air sermons to thousands of people thirsty for spiritual solace and hope.

His brother Charles wrote many hymns including *Hark The Herald Angels Sing* and *Love Divine All Love Excelling*.

John Milton was buried in the ancient church of St Giles Cripplegate.

The present building overlooks The Barbican. Milton is probably still trying to *"justify the ways of God to man"* and defend our freedom of speech, sorely in need of defending today.

Oliver Cromwell married his first wife in the church.

Just down the road John Donne stands in a marbled winding sheet on a plinth in St Paul's, a scorch mark on the gown marking the statue's survival of the Great Fire of London of 1666; "when London burnt like rotten sticks."

He wrote the lines *"Death Be Not Proud though some have called thee Mighty and dreadfull"* and the stirring exhortation *"Batter my Heart three persone'd God for you as yet but knocke, breathe, shine and seek to mend."*

Such language stirs my soul and mind and I think I'd follow such writers into any battle, physical or moral.

Shakespeare lived in Ireland Street. His signature is on a mortgage document in the Guildhall Museum. His involvement with The Curtain and The Theatre in Shoreditch, led to the pulling down by stealth of The Theatre by Richard Burbage and Shakespeare and then taking the wood across to the other side of the Thames to build The Globe. It burnt down in 1613 during a performance of Henry the Eighth when theatrical cannon misfired, sending sparks into the wooden beams and the thatching.

Over three hundred and fifty years later, I went to an exhibition of the plans for a new Globe. Whilst looking at a model I fell into conversation with Sam Wanamaker, the Canadian actor whose dream it had been and whose drive and energy had led to the project becoming close to reality. He was a charming man with strong charisma.

As he spoke he became more excited and I sparked off from his enthusiasm.

Our conversation led to my promising to help raise more money for the project.

I got involved in Elizabethan dancing and also took groups for a tour of Westminster Abbey and St Paul's Cathedral. So in a way I am part of the Globe's history.

Next to the Globe is the house Christopher Wren lived in and after a day toiling over his plans, he could see his masterpiece, St Paul's Cathedral rising from the ashes.

His epitaph in the crypt says *"Lector, si monumentum requires, circumspice"*
"Reader, if you seek his monument, look around you."

Samuel Pepys, lecher, diarist and Secretary to the Navy sat on the leads of his house in Seething Lane near the Tower Of London in the summer evenings and sang to the accompaniment of a lute.

He's buried in St Olave's Church in Hart Street round the corner.
Walter Raleigh felt the edge of the axe in front of Westminster Hall before his execution and remarked that it *"was a sharp medicine to cure all my ills."*
This is my City. When it rains and the wind howls through the alleyways of the City

I pretend I am William Shakespeare on the way to the Globe across the river.

I hunch my shoulders, bow my head, skip from doorway to doorway, muttering *"Now is the winter of our discontent*

Made glorious by this sun of York."

I studied the City, its history, the Roman influence and became a part time guide of its hidden secrets and obscure passages.

Getting off the Tube at the Embankment I feel a frisson of excitement even now.

Good Bye Sheila

It was a phone call on a Sunday morning that told me Sheila was dead.

Blessing was sobbing down the phone and I told her I would come straight over to her house.

Sheila and Edith had been on their tandem coming from Shooters Hill when a lorry hit them side on smashing the tandem in two. Sheila had been killed instantly. Edith was in intensive care in Greenwich Hospital. We sat in the sitting room with silent neighbours and Blessing nursing Toby the Jack Russell. She kept saying

"It's alright Tobes." I looked at the book shelf and gave quiet thanks to this lovely lady who had had such an influence on my life. The garden was in full bloom and a light breeze was causing the trees to sway and send different shades of light across the lawn. I thought of that day I had seen Edith and Sheila locked in a loving embrace. The vision made me smile and cry. Blessing called the hospital and was told Edith was too ill to be seen.

We buried Sheila the following week. Blessing asked me to say something at the funeral. I spoke of the great love Sheila had had for Blessing.

I told the mourners of the indelible effect she had had on my life, intellectually and emotionally. I praised her partnership with Edith as delicately as possible.

A staunch and constant companion I called her. As the curtain started to close and Sheila to disappear we played a tape of *Daisy Daisy Give me your answer do, I'm half crazy all for the love of you. We won't have a stylish marriage, I can't afford the carriage but you'll look sweet upon the seat of a bicycle made for two.*

Sheila had left a will in which she had asked that a drinks party be held at her home and laughter should be the theme. We did our best, though tears predominated and burst through our smiling facades. Edith was too ill to come.

We went to see her at the hospital. It was a shock. Her face was battered and bruised and all sorts of tubes were attached to her body. She managed a whispered hello and then indicated we should draw nearer

"I know maybe I shouldn't ask this but… can I be buried next to Sheila?" Blessing said immediately

"Of course dear Edith, but try and get better."

Edith died two days later. It was just us, a few neighbours, and former work colleagues. A representative from the Girl Guides was there. I spoke again and thanked Edith for imparting her knowledge of gardens to me and of supporting Blessing and Sheila in all their endeavours. This time we played the Ink Spots singing *Into Each Life Some Rain Must Fall*

On the way home Blessing suddenly said to me,

"I wonder how many people knew they were lovers, don't you?"

I smiled. "Yes. I'll miss them so much."

"You know that I'm…"

"Oh yes."

We hugged each other.

London Library

"A great many people now reading and writing would be better employed keeping rabbits." – Edith Sitwell.
"When I want to read a novel I write one." – Benjamin Disraeli

The London Library was founded in 1841 and sometimes I feel the ghosts of past members walking past or nodding off in a chair in the Reading Room.

Is that Charles Dickens sitting there or maybe Thackeray, Gladstone, Disraeli or Dame Rebecca West?

Large sums of money have been spent recently modernising and adding more space. A donation of £2.5 million from Valerie Eliot, widow of T.S Eliot was of major importance; and of course my £200.

In the older parts of the Library there are gloomy narrow stacks lit by neon lighting that give off shocks when I switch one on.

I have problems these days finding the "y"s and "w"s which are often at the bottom of the shelves and repair to a librarian to appeal for help whilst pathetically holding my long suffering back. Scruffy little desks appear in dusty corners for consultation and note taking. I mainly pre-order from the electronic catalogue and then when on a visit trawl through the collection, often finding by chance, a gem to borrow.

The Library is not a treasure trove for sports books, but I have found Teach Tennant and Drobny in there.

My routine is to collect the ordered books and go through them in the Reading Room, checking I really want to read them. The Reading Room is a large room with windows overlooking St James' Square. Five foot mahogany bases support flat four sided Corinthian columns that in turn support the ceiling where hang thin brass chandeliers with white globes. Iron stairs carry one upstairs to a walkway where on the shelves are hundreds of reference books and dictionaries. A few reading stands lean over from the balcony, made of iron and oak. Down stairs I sit at a table desk with inlaid leather to make notes and write surrounded by industrious scribblers and somnolent armchair readers nodding off as a book slips from their hand. A Victorian marble fireplace with iron interior and a small pole screen is in a corner which again sets my imagination off, the thought of Wilkie Collins and Carlisle, the founder sitting roasting their feet on a foggy London day.

Large stands with deep sleeves contain journals and magazines of every conceivable subject stamped with the admonition "Not to be taken away" take up more space

Swing doors lead to a computer room where one can consult the catalogue.

Another swing door takes the member to the Victorian Urinals with modern ones down another staircase.

The big reception area is staffed usually with four or five librarians taking and receiving books for stamping or return,

The atmosphere is orderly and quiet. Mobiles are supposed to be strictly forbidden but the usual crass bores sit on the stairs braying into their phones.

There is a room to eat sandwiches and make coffee but I usually buy a baguette and coffee and sit in the charming St James Square Garden amongst the plane trees and office workers, even on cold days.

I often think of Sheila and Blessing when I am there and in the Library.

I love the place.

Cats

Do not meddle in the affairs of cats for they are subtle and will piss on your computer.

If you don't like cats turn over the next few pages.

My wife Karen and my daughters Tessa and Sophie are besotted, silly, foolish and in love with all cats. They truly believe the little wonders understand every word they say. On holiday in Crete, my wife will feed ten or more of the wild ones who always come to our door. A walk down the road is interrupted whilst she strokes or admires a cat. Any cat sitting in a window is treated to "oohs" and "aahs."

They all make silly voices expressing their love for the creatures.

Tessa worries our lot will have no-one to talk to when we go on holiday.

I, of course, can take cats or leave them.

Over the years we have had Eboli, named after the putative villainess of Verdi's opera Don Carlos who wore an eye patch. She was white with a black patch over one eye. She came to us via the cat flap, a little affectionate purring bundle and stayed for eighteen years. If anybody sneezed she wrinkled her nose and sneezed back.

She had no problem opening the fridge door and scattering food all over the kitchen floor. Karen devised a rubber band to prevent her depredations into our supper.

Macavity, a black and at times surly fellow, survived until nineteen. At six o'clock he would start to tap his bowl just as Karen came in from work.

His sister Minky was a tortoiseshell who spread her whole body over the front of anybody who didn't mind. She made it until seventeen. We took her to the vet and watched her gentle death injection. We left and staggered down the street, bereaved and weeping.

We now have four. Two older ones, a black and white brother and sister garnered from the Cat Protection League called Rosy and Jimbo. The younger ones have been adopted from my daughter Tessa. Larry is a tiger-like grey tabby and Yoshi a divine tortoiseshell.

Sophie, my daughter in Oxford sends us daily reports on her two black cats Bunk and Boo. She has made her partner, Gary, as besotted as she is. I also have to listen to their purrs on the phone. When I hear a really concerned note in my wife's voice whilst talking to Sophie I know that one of her cats has gone missing, is puking up all over the kitchen or is not eating its food and so on.

Yoshi is shy and cautious and not a lap cat. She spends a lot of time in the alleyway next to our house mewing at and being stroked by the children on their way to and from school. She has taken to visiting two gay ladies in the next street who deny vehemently that they are feeding her. The rest of the time she is on someone's bed or the rocking chair in the lounge.

Larry is the mafia thug and enforcer and terrorises the others, especially his sister, the gangster's moll Yoshi. He comes charging in at supper time as if from some great cat plain beyond the garden wall. He pretends to act as a lap cat, albeit very jumpy and choosey. Just as you think he has settled he moves to someone else's lap.

At supper time he struts around deciding from which bowl he will deign to eat from whilst the others keep a wary eye on him. Most of his day is spent sleeping on the trampoline next door or in one of the flower beds. He has pigeon hunting days and is quite successful. He delights in bringing in frogs and laying them at our feet.

Karen always rescues them and returns them to the wild.

I think he brings the same ones back often.

For whatever reason he makes us laugh just to look at him.

Jimbo is being renamed Jumbo as his weight goes up all the time. He will start proselytising for food from early morning until late at night.

No bowl is safe and he hoovers up all food left by the others He likes to fight with me. As I sit reading he will jump onto the arm of the chair and head-butt me.

I retaliate with a heavy stroking of the lower part of his back which sends him into a pretend frenzy. He threshes back and forth, usually finally losing his footing and falling into my chair. When he first came, he ignored all pleadings to sit on a lap. Now he jumps up and takes his rights of being hugged and settles down for an intimate purring conversation, basically about food.

Rosie. Oh my Rosy. This cat reminds me of Sally. She is more like a dog than a cat.

She is sitting as I write on a pile of my notes and from time to time wipes out several thousand words by walking across the computer. She has a mad few moments every day when the world is boring her. Rosy comes a little way out of the bedroom where she spends hours on a chair or the bed and like a burglar casing the joint, peers down the hall. A crazy look descends and she races into our study doing a circuit including behind a red cabinet, a chicane around the sofa and then charges back to the bedroom. She repeats this several times. At night as soon as I prepare to go upstairs, she rushes up in front of me and sits outside whilst I am in the bathroom, scratching the door and meowing.

The ritual continues with a piece of string pulled back and forth across the bed or over the rail which she leaps at. I put it under the sheet and entice her in and then throw the sheet over her. She wrestles all over the bed before shooting out from the side. The morning ritual is for her to arrive with my tea, make a little prp prp sound as she jumps onto the bed, stretches out a gentle paw towards my face, tries to push the morning paper aside and prepares for her head rub.

Each side of the head must be attended to and if I stop, she nudges her head under my hand ordering me to resume. All this action culminates in a retreat to the end of the bed and a flop down, peeking back at me through her paws. The only way she will sit on a lap is by the placing of a cushion between her and the lap. Any cat who has claimed a seat to sleep on, even my favourite Chestnut Windsor chair is never turfed off. Gentle hands are placed under the cushion and the cat is transferred without any disturbance to a free chair, still in deep sleep.

If our cats had mobiles, Rosy's ringtone would be prp prp, Jimbo's heavy purring. Larry's, a growl and meow, Yoshi's a light mewing.

Every day a conversation takes place between Karen and Tessa on where each cat spent the night. Was it the lounge downstairs? Or the spare room bed? On the kitchen chair? On the end of my bed?

No discussion of cats can be complete without their food consumption.

"Has Larry been in yet?" asks Tessa as if he has been out all night on patrol.

"Rosie's not happy with the tuna and haddock combination."

"Yoshi's still on the bed and Jimbo wants more."

My mother gave our cats whatever was left over from our meals. They supplemented any shortfall with mice, birds and the next door neighbour's rubbish bin.

My family have extensive and serious discussions on our cats' needs.

Because the modern urban cat is incapable of serious hunting because he or she is too fat, too lazy, too spoilt, then the relative merits of their cat pouches are of enormous interest. Some members of our tribe will not eat anything with fish. Others ignore any beef or lamb mixtures. When I trail behind Karen or Tessa at the supermarket, I stand in a trance thinking of whether Alastair Cook and Strauss will put on another record breaking opener's score. Whilst the merits of Whiskas or Felix, dry food and how many pouches are needed are being assessed, Pietersen has scored his first double century in Test matches against Australia and Swann has taken eight for thirty.

My duty is to dutifully carry the two forty eight pouches per carton to the car. Often anguished phone calls from Sophie centre on Bunk and Boo's refusal of special offer rabbit and salmon pouches with Gary weeping in the back ground.

I often, well sometimes, well seldom, question the cost of looking after these cats; vets, food, collars, special dry food, vaccinations.

Each time I am forced to concede that they more than pay for their keep with their comforting and entertaining presence.

Elegy for Jimbo

Jimbo has been in decline for several weeks. Serious loss of weight had led to a diagnosis from the vet of imminent death from diabetes. I went into denial or at least thinking that he could be loved and cared for at home and might be able to die in dignity in the kitchen chair he was currently favouring. Sadly after a family conference we agreed we couldn't allow him to suffer and we took him to the vet.

On a dark wet evening, we placed him in the cat basket and in sombre mood entered the surgery. A young and kind vet explained that there were no alternatives he could offer. We stood weeping whilst he administered the final injection. We stroked a purring Jimbo's head to the last moment and our beloved Jimbo was gone.

People who don't like animals say to you as you weep, "but it's only a cat. Human beings are more important."

It depends on the human being.

Part Seven

"And I have asked to be
Where no storms come
Where the green swell is in the haven dumb
And out of the swing of the sea."
Gerald Manley Hopkins

Boulogne and The Final Triumph

I finally got permission from Wilson to take Blessing to meet him. He asked if I could take Thelma.

I took the usual precautions, taking a bus into the countryside and then walking the rest of the way, blindfolding Blessing for the last few miles and carrying Thelma carefully in her basket. As I had guessed, Blessing and Wilson took to each other straight away. Wilson had just got back from a long trip where he had run marathons on the Great Wall of China, Antarctica, and the North Pole.

He had also competed for the first time in the Comrades.

It was Blessing's dream to compete in this race. It takes place in the Kwazulu-Natal Province of South Africa and is an endurance test of the body and mind. Its credo. "to celebrate mankind's spirit over adversity."

Along its 90 km route there are cut off points for those failing to keep the pace necessary to finish in under twelve hours. Wilson who was I think about eighty four then had emulated the South African first world war veteran Wally Hayward who had finished the course at age eighty one in 1989.

Hayward had won the race five times, the last time at age forty five. Wilson had devastated the field winning in four hours and fifteen seconds. On his way back to England he had run and won the Boston Marathon in one hour and ten minutes.

Blessing asked him to help her with a training and diet programme that would enable her to run marathons and eventually The Comrades. A gleam came into his eyes.

"I will my dear but first I have a plan for Ricky, you, myself and one other to take part in a historic race."

"Tell me, tell me."

"Be patient. First I have to ask a big favour of Someone."

"Who's the other person?"

"That is the subject of the favour."

We went for a run across the moor and then plunged into the icy river. A race back to the cave was won easily by Wilson and we crawled into the sleeping bags Blessing had packed whilst Wilson roasted the green beans and shallots in sea salt and olive oil I had brought with us from London. He looked as fit as ever in the light of the fire and I wondered how Big J would deal with his old age. When would Wilson be considered old?

He looked up and smiled at me as if he knew what I was thinking.

"Long way to go Ricky, my friend.

Did you know that Virgil was considered an honorary Christian by the Church?"

"No"

"Virgil forecast a saviour in a poem. He wrote;

"He will foregather with the Gods… the waving corn will slowly flood the plains with gold, grapes hang in ruby clusters and honey dew exude from the hard trunk of the oak, perfumes of Assyria will breathe from every hedge."

"Let me tell you a story, a true story about the origin of the Marathon.

Pheidippedes was a Greek soldier born round about 490 B.C. His speciality was as a messenger for the Army because of his prodigious stamina.

When the Greeks finally defeated the Persians, Pheidippides was ordered to run from Marathon to Athens to announce the victory. He had to run around Mount Pentelli and across rough terrain. He made it but at the cost of his life. He had run without stopping for over twenty miles. He entered the Assembly and shouted, "We have won," collapsed and died.

Today over five hundred marathons a year are run.

Think of that story when I contact you."

I left Thelma with Wilson. A week or so later, she arrived home looking very fit, the distance from Yorkshire was like a flight in the park for her.

The message was to get hold of Blessing and sit in the garden with her on the following Sunday at three o'clock. Blessing was by now a representative for a sports company often accompanying sports stars on their journeys. But her love of running was part of her make-up and she ran every day.

I held her hand and waited for the familiar whoosh.

When we opened our eyes, Peter was waiting. As ever he was grumpy.

He didn't really approve of visitors, especially women, but finally unlocked the Gates (they're not Pearly by the way) stamped our special visas and ushered us through.

We went to the Elysian Fields Sports area where Wilson was waiting.

A slim soldierly looking figure came toward us.

"Meet Pheidippides" said Wilson. Blessing nearly fainted. He was on a temporary secondment from Olympus. He smiled modestly and invited us to drink from the sparkling waters. Wilson laid out his plan. All four of us were to repeat the famous run at a date convenient to us all.

Blessing was beside herself with excitement. I was more circumspect and Pheidippides said he wasn't sure his legs would stand up to the challenge.

We were joined by a professor of exercise physiology, Dr Gossens.

The authorities were keen to promote the slowing down of the ageing process, he said.

The Heavens were getting crowded and there were fears of problems if too many people kept arriving. Blessing laughed. "We've got the opposite problem on Earth. Not enough people leaving, dropping dead." Dr Gossens, a fit looking man with a droopy moustache and a humorous visage said, "The goal posts had been moved on the definition of old age. Humans are specifically adapted to take part in strenuous muscular activity. The ability to run for hours of endurance effort came from running down game animals. People don't even run for abus now."

In the past, Marathon runners like Dorando Pietri in the 1908 Olympics collapsed close to the finishing line or Jim Peters who lost a three mile lead in the Commonwealth Games of Vancouver in 1954. They were dehydrated.

That wouldn't happen today unless they ignored all advice and the bottles of water offered on the route."

"What about Paula Radcliffe?"

Dr Gossens took a deep breath. "I yield to no-one in my admiration for that woman. She had serious asthma and anaemia as a child yet fought to be allowed to run in competitions. At the Olympics in 2004 she had been taking anti-inflammatory drugs for an injured leg. Her advisers failed to realise that the drugs were hindering her food absorption which of course caused lack of energy and loss of carbohydrates.

Yet look how she came back to win more races and titles."

"How did that happen?", Blessing asked.

"Human nature in its unpredictability continues to confound the experts. One sports scientist predicts a two hour marathon, or around 1.58."

Wilson said, "Two of the most important factors are the economy of the runner, the amount of energy expended whilst running. A really good runner will use thirty percent less energy than an average runner. Another reason might be an ability to consume oxygen at higher rates without producing much lactic acid.

This is where the indefinable enters the equation. Cliché it may be but mind over matter can conquer mountains. Look how you won your Wimbledon title Ricky.

You had heart problems, a sore back. Yet you were determined not to give quarter or flinch from the fray. Dr Gossens doesn't know, neither do I where that extra strength and bravery comes from. We should probably ask Big J."

Dr Gossens said "We are hoping that sort of courage will inspire the people of the West to change their life styles. From up here we see Tweedle Dums and Tweedle Dees waddling along and many of the fatties are young people. Their bottoms can't fit into chairs or on toilet seats. They start to sweat and smell. They can't run, work or help society. The weekend alcohol bingers and their bloated bodies and faces are an affront to the efforts of doctors and health professionals to make people aware of the damage they do to their own bodies and the tears and recriminations they bring on their families as they face early decline and death. Despite improved techniques to counter obesity, the services are being overwhelmed. In Britain they try stomach stapling, fitting gastric bands and inserting a "bubble" to fill the stomach up.

We have figures of over one billion overweight adults, world wide.

Stanley Matthews loped by on his training run and we beckoned him over.

He had played his last game for England aged forty two and his last competitive game at age seventy. "I slowed down the ageing process for myself by the way I lived.

I was a vegetarian, teetotal, and a non smoker. Yes I know I advertised for "Craven A" cigarettes but I needed the money.

My Dad had been a top boxer, known as "The Fighting Barber of Hanley" and had instilled discipline into me from a young age. I used to get up at dawn and stand before the open window doing deep breathing exercises. I did special exercises to keep my muscles flexible.

Don't forget we had a different life in those days. I helped in my dad's barber shop, and then started an apprenticeship as a bricklayer. When I first started at Stoke as an office boy I walked eight miles to work, except when it was snowing.

Then Mum would give me the fare for the bus. When I played at Blackpool during my army service I ran along Blackpool beach and plunged into the icy water as part of my keep fit regime. You know Ricky too how in team games you can use your skills in a different way as you get older.

"You learn to read the game differently and to conserve your energies. I went back to Stoke aged forty six and played there until I was fifty.

I always think I retired too early."

It's hard to explain to the modern generation how famous Stanley was.

People who had no interest in football knew who he was.

In foreign lands, to say "Stanley Matthews" was to break the communication barrier.

Thousands of people lined the way of his funeral cortege with bowed heads and tears in their eyes. His ashes were buried beneath the centre circle of the Britannia Stadium ground. The epitaph on his statue outside the ground speaks of;

"A magical player of the people, for the people." He was never booked or sent off.

Perhaps the greatest tribute of all came from Pele;

"The man who taught us the way football should be played."

By now we were attracting attention from other people on the field.

Joe Louis and Max Schemeling were sparring and grunting but keeping an ear on the conversation. They lumbered over. Max looked magnificent, like an old ravaged lion at bay and continued to bob and weave as he spoke.

"I think I was always naturally fit but of course I slowed down with age.

In those days we drank and smoked and didn't look to the long term did we Joe?"

Joe has some problems with focussing and took his time in answering.

"I spent too much of my time fighting the Inland Revenue and racism.

Max helped me out a lot, despite the fact I whupped him in New York the second time we fought."

"Don't forget you dropped me with an illegal kidney punch Joe."

"Yeh you was robbed Max."

They both agreed that the continual pummelling to the body and the punches to the head inevitably take their toll and the punishment a heavy weight boxer takes makes it certain that age finishes their careers.

"You always fight one fight too far which finishes you.

Look at Muhammed Ali," said Max. Joe cited George Forman who fought a World Heavyweight fight against Michael Moorer at age forty five.

Forman retired at forty eight. I looked at Joe and thought of all the Brown Bomber had been through. His father had been part white, his mother half Cherokee. Joe grew up in a virulently racist society and learnt to deal with "White Folks" by being what Ali called ignorantly an, "Uncle Tom."

He served in a segregated cavalry unit and was promoted to Sergeant.

It suited the hypocritical fight organisers to bill his fights with Max as the Nazi versus the clean living and upright American even though he couldn't eat or drink in white bars or travel on trains and buses in the same carriages as the whites.

He was pursued throughout his career by a vindictive Inland Revenue Service and ended up as a "Meeter" and "Greeter" in a Las Vegas hotel before really going down hill with drink and drugs. In one of his finer moments Ronald Reagan waived eligibility rules so Joe could be buried at Arlington which was paid for partly by Max. Max was a pall bearer. Joe was buried with full military honours.

On his tomb is a bas relief of him and the epitaph, "The Brown Bomber."

Three volleys were fired in tribute to his memory.

Both men sat quietly in thought, obviously comfortable with their reminiscences.

I asked Max how he had dealt with the "Nazi" label when he went to the States.

A spark of anger lit up his eyes.

"I never joined the Nazi Party. I was never an anti-Semite."

"But you were born in 1905 so by the time Hitler came to power you were already twenty eight. Surely you were aware of his and his party's policies."

"For sure, but I had lived through the Great Depression, political assassinations, the Weimar Republic. I was young and life became sweet as I progressed my boxing career.

The girls!

If I walked into a night club in Berlin I was given free champagne, food and as many women as I wanted. Who knew about the plan to murder the Jews and occupy Eastern Europe?

"But what of the Nuremberg Laws, Kristalnacht, the efforts to get rid of all the Jews?

The fanatical speeches of Hitler and Goebbels at Nazi rallies?"

Max was quiet and looked thoughtful.

"Look you know I sheltered two Jewish boys and helped them to get out of Germany."

"But you joined the Luftwaffe."

Max was getting edgy and pushed his face close to mine.

"I was a paratrooper in the Luftwaffe. Hitler hated me for refusing to join the Party. Yes I was a patriot, loved my country like many others. Germany had been humiliated at Versailles when I was thirteen years of age.

I went through the Great Depression and saw my father weeping and burning a pile of useless currency whilst my mother wrung her hands. My father never let me forget those days. Let me ask you a question. If you had been in my position, famous, fit and becoming rich but living in England and Hitler had invaded and defeated the British do you think you would have resisted being feted by him?

Do you think the British people would have listened to the blandishments of the anti- Semites or fought to the death, for the last piece of soil?"

I had no answer.

Max continued. "I don't think so. There were many anti-Semites in Britain especially amongst the upper classes. People like that Mitford girl and her circle.

The Duke of Windsor was a traitor and should have been executed in the Tower of London."

He sank back in to his chair. I turned to Joe.

"What did you make of being called an Uncle Tom, collaborating with white men to present a false image?"

Joe looked at Max and grinned.

"Where's this boy coming from? I had nothing to fight with. The race laws ruled over all of us blacks. The hatred shown by whites to us especially in the South was an abomination. When I fought against Max they accepted me for the night as an athlete. I was a man in the ring but called a boy in the street. The *United Press* boxing man wrote that I was, *"a jungle man, completely primitive as any savage"* "Protesting got us a beating. The back of the bus was our place until those brave people; both black and white came along in the 1960's.

I was only twenty one when they lynched Rubin Stacey. He was a poor uneducated homeless boy who went begging door to door. The Sheriff took him into custody. The upstanding church going white citizens broke into the jail. Took Rubin away and lynched him. They were so pleased with themselves they took photographs and distributed them. No-one was prosecuted. White folk sent post cards to friends in other states of lynchings of blacks. It became a big industry for the USA Postal Services.

Our great and noble President Franklin Delano Roosevelt would not support a federal anti-lynching bill. Four young share croppers were lynched in 1946 including a World War Two veteran. No-one was prosecuted. A man fights for his country, bothers no-one and dies mutilated and his neck broken while pasty faced white men bay for more blood.

You think I should have been protesting?

I became a good golfer and in 1952 the only way I could test how good I was, was to be infiltrated on a technicality into a PGA tournament.

If I had ever refused to serve in the Army like Muhammed Ali and said "No Vietcong ever called me nigger," I would have been lynched.

Don't ask me about being an Uncle Tom."

I was stunned and felt humiliated.

How ignorant I had been of those times and mores.

How could I understand such venomous barbarities?

They didn't seem to bear me any ill-will, mock sparred with me and slouched off with their arms around each other.

As I sat pondering my words, Fanny Blankers Koen ran by with Emil and waved regally and gave a big smile to Blessing.

"You used to be me."

Emil pointed at me,

"And you used to be me."

Everybody laughed. Fanny said

"Don't forget Wilson, I was pregnant when I won my four medals in 1948. Beat that superman."

Wilson bowed and reminded us of Nicole Brakebusch-Leveque who ran a marathon in the European 1998 championships at age forty seven and of Martina winning her final title at the US Open Tennis at age fifty.

With tongue in cheek I reminded Wilson that Thelma was nine years of age, very old for a racing pigeon.

Blessing was dying with impatience to learn more about the proposed Marathon.

We had a discussion with Pheidippides who was going back to Olympus to start training. He would do stamina work with Heracles and promised to refrain from hanging out with Dionysus at the Olympus Tavern. He would meet us in Greece, his travel arrangements to be organised by Helios. We were intrigued by this revelation.

"Helios drives his four horse chariot daily across the Heavens from his palace in Colchis and then returns by boat across the Ocean stream taking his chariot and team on a golden ferry boat."

"I'd love to do that" exclaimed Blessing.

Pheidippides confessed it would be a new experience for him and he had made sure Phaeton, Helios' son wouldn't be part of the team. "When the young fool was given the chance to drive the sun chariot, Phaeton had driven it so high above the earth that he scorched the fields."

"And the angry Zeus had killed him with a thunderbolt", I said

"Oh yes but he had been forgiven and reborn."

Wilson and we two were enthralled and wanted to know more about Pheidippides.

"I was always involved in sport as a child. Greek children were encouraged to take part in every type of physical exercise. My father had been a soldier and I was to follow his example. He said a young man should develop his body's strength to be able to endure all efforts, however strenuous. He took me to the sports stadium and enrolled me in the Pentathlon which was part of Army training.

First I practiced discus throwing.

"Show us", said Blessing.

Pheidippides picked up a stone shaped like a flying saucer.

"Try it."

Blessing wound herself up and hurled the discus with all her strength into the distance. "Not bad. Run and get it, will you?"

He took the disc from a puffing Blessing.

"You are making the mistake of confusing strength with the real attributes needed. Watch. It is a combination of rhythm and precision." In one graceful movement and without any apparent major effort, Pheidippides hurled the discus way into the distance.

"The javelin needs the same care and discipline. In our time the pole was the height of an average man, about five feet seven inches, with an attached metal point and a thong for the hurler's fingers attached to its centre of gravity.

Next was the Jump. Come on Wilson, you know about this."

Wilson picked up a stone weight to our surprise. He measured out a distance and then solemnly stood waiting for Pheidippides to give him the word. He took off and as he came down used his arms and the stone behind his back to propel his body further.

"Well done, you might even have beaten me in the old days.

Now Ricky, how are your wrestling powers?"

"What!".

"Throw me to the ground making sure I land on my hip, shoulder or back for a fair fall. No come on, I won't resist, it is just to teach you."

I managed with great difficulty to throw Pheidippides, whilst Blessing and Wilson, wreathed in smiles shouted encouragement.

"It needs three falls for victory and there must be no biting or holding of genitals."

Blessing grinned "I'm glad about that."

"But you are allowed to break your opponent's fingers."

The final discipline was running.

"We had four types of racing. A 192 metres sprint, a three hundred and eighty four metres and one thousand three hundred and forty four metres races.

"You said four races."

"Correct. The fourth was the killer. Three hundred and eighty four metres but this time dressed in armour."

"What sort of armour?"

"I wore a helmet, shield and greaves, great bronze plates worn on the legs and thighs.

This race was specifically included to increase speed and stamina for entrance into military service. They weighed about fifty to sixty pounds."

"What was your childhood like?".

"I came from Penteli, which was famous for its marble. As you know it was used later for the Parthenon, which was before my time I'm afraid.

It was a flawless white with a faint yellow tint which made it shine with a golden glow in the sunlight. My grandfather worked in the quarries and so did my father before he became a soldier and we moved around a bit then."

"Long after your time, Penteli was the site of terrible forest fires" I said.

"Yes: in 1995, 1998 to 2001, and again in 2007.

We never experienced anything like that in my time. We lived well, had good food and wine. After school I went straight to the sports field and became a renowned runner."

"Did you really run all those miles to Athens and back?" said Wilson.

Pheidippides laughed "You know what they say. When faced with the truth or the legend, print the legend. No, we went on horseback, picking up fresh horses on the way. But the Marathon story is basically true; certainly my death was not misreported.

I went westwards along the eastern and northern slopes of Mount Pentelli, the pass of Dionysus. Unfortunately I didn't meet him until after I died. We've had a few nights out since then. He can drink anyone under the table.

From the pass I went straight downhill to Athens, in all I would guess about twenty two miles. I remember on the downhill run I was feeling exhausted with a pain in my chest. I was vaguely aware of collapsing and crying,

"The victory is ours."

When I arrived in Olympus, Asclepius was summoned to ascertain the cause of death.

Heart failure was his diagnosis."

"The immortal Asclepius" said Blessing

"Not quite. He was the son of Apollo but his mother was a mortal so he died a human death. He was killed at one time by a thunderbolt from a moody Zeus but was reborn later." Pheidippides looked around and lowered his voice.

"I must be discreet in this place. Asclepius had the gifts of healing the injured, the blind and sick and even the raising of the dead."

"But please be discreet, not a word to Big J. I mustn't tread on his toes."

"Our lips are sealed."

Our time was up. We said farewell to Pheidippides, grabbed the rail and were whisked to the departure point and waited to be sent down.

Our appetite for running had been wetted.

I decided to travel down to Dorset to see an old acquaintance.

Sydney Wooderson

Sydney Wooderson was one of the greatest ever of British athletes.
I had been with my mother as a young boy in 1945 when a fifty four thousand crowd broke down the gates at White City to see the race between Sydney and Arne Andersson, the Swedish champion. I was frightened of the crowd but a tall man and his gangly son protected my mother and me from the crush. The boy's name was Roger Bannister, a polite quiet sort of chap who became vociferous when the race started. Sydney, nicknamed the Mighty Atom had held the world record for the mile in 1937.

He was the most unlikely athlete ever seen. Five foot six and weighing nine stone his hair was brylcreemed and his short sighted eyes peered through black horn rimmed glasses He had skinny white legs and wore baggy all black kit.

He took record after record as a school boy and trained as a solicitor, missing the 1938 Empire Games in Australia to take his law exams.

At Motspur Park in 1937 a handicap race had been arranged for him to see if he could capture the record. The officials found out just in time that the track was two inches short and adjusted Wooderson's position accordingly.

Reg Thomas, a good runner himself set out ten yards in front and others were given various yardages. Sydney's brother was allotted one hundred and forty yards in front. Wooderson ran the first lap in fifty eight point six seconds; at the half mile the time was just over two minutes. Sydney then got boxed in and detoured into the outside lane to discover no runners to incentivise him in front. He ploughed on and took the tape in four minutes six point four seconds, a new world record.

I had pictures of him in my scrap book being carried shoulder high from the track, his mother and father cheering and beaming in the background.

At White City eight years later Sydney who had served in The Pioneer Corp and REME, and suffered a severe illness, was not quite up to the strength of Andersson, and was beaten into second place. My new friend Roger said he loved the dignity of Sydney and his attitude to running.

"It was a good thing in itself and not just to win trophies."

Another admirer said that Sydney Wooderson epitomised the Greek ideal of perseverance, self discipline and grace of movement.

Roger went on to become a distinguished neurologist and the first man to break the four minute barrier in the mile. He once said that every morning in Africa, a gazelle wakes up. It knows it must out-run the fastest lion or be killed. Every morning in Africa a lion wakes up and knows it must out-run the slowest gazelle or starve.

It doesn't matter whether you are a lion or gazelle, when the sun comes up you'd better be running. Of that day we shared at White City he said he was inspired to pursue his running dreams by the sight of this unprepossessing man with spindly legs and glasses concentrating and stretching himself to the limit of his strength.

I had met Sydney through Blackheath Harriers, a venerable athletics club first brought into being at The Green Man, Blackheath in the nineteenth century. He had stayed close to the club all his life and came along to train and encourage any body at any level. A very modest and charming man, he knew I was never going to be the steeple chaser I aspired to but never said a word, just kept quietly encouraging me. Over cups of tea in the clubhouse we found we shared a passion for jazz. Especially at that time so-called traditional jazz and skiffle were popular.

At the Hot Club of Woolwich, he had seen Chris Barber with his wife, the fabulous blues singer Ottilie Patterson. I still have an old seventy eight of her singing *Make Me A Pallet On The Floor*. Ken Colyer sang *Going Home*, a reference to his release from a New Orleans jail for possession of marijuana. Humphrey Lyttleton, with the outrageous George Melly doing his *Frankie and Johnny* act when at the end of the song he fell dramatically "shot" to the stage floor. The banjo player in Chris Barber's band sang *Rock Island Line, John Henry* and went on to be the famous Lonnie Donegan with such hits as

Does Your Chewing Gum Lose Its Flavour on the Bed Post Over Night? and, *My Old Man's a Dustman*.

Sydney introduced me to Charlie Parker, Chet Baker, Thelonius Monk and the sublime Miles Davis. We then moved onto singers like the Divine Sarah, Ella, Nina Simone, Peggy Lee, Mahalia Jackson, Lena Horne and a host of others.

Over the years we kept in touch, so it was good to see him again snug and happy in his Dorset cottage with his wife Pamela. He walked four miles everyday.

I wanted to stir his memory and get some tips on training for running.

"You need to run long distances as much as you can whether you are training for one hundred yards or the marathon. Macdonald Bailey was one of the most dedicated trainers I ever knew and he won national championships and an Olympic Medal.

He once raced against the hare at White City to test himself."

"Do you think the mind, the will, is as important as the ability to run fast?"

"Yes I do. In my first mile run ever as a schoolboy, the boy standing next to me set off at such a fast pace, it startled us all. He was taller and older than me. I stuck doggedly behind him and each time he increased his pace, I kept as close as possible. I was gasping for breath, my head spinning but I wouldn't let him go.

He kept looking over his shoulder and I could see in his eyes the gleam of doubt.

With about twenty yards to go I summoned every last vestige of strength and overhauled him.

We had both broken the school record."

"Tell me the story of the 1948 Olympics in London."

"Oh that old story again. I was scheduled to have the honour of being the last runner into the stadium with a torch and light the Olympic flame. Athletics in those days, like tennis, rugby and football was run by ghastly old farts in blazers with gold buttons and club ties, who had done something or other in the war, got medals and sinecures on committees. Most of them had no history of sporting prowess or battle honours. My particular bête noire was Commander Bill Collins, a rotund, pink cheeked gin and tonic soaked waffler.

He and the committee decided I wasn't handsome enough to represent my country, my athletic record and my army service apparently meaningless. I found out even the Queen agreed. "Of course we couldn't have had poor little Sydney." So that was that.

I won the National Cross Country that same year as a final gesture to the establishment and got an MBE fifty years later."

This giant of an athlete and human being was awarded an MBE when most people had forgotten him.

It is an apt comment on our obsequious and infantile society.

Michael Caine threatens to leave the country if Margaret Thatcher is defeated and his taxes go up.

Sean Connery is a member of the Scottish National Party and lives abroad.

They both agitate and bleat for knighthoods and get them. Archer, a Knight of the post, a man who gave false evidence, perjured himself and goes to prison as does Conrad Black, yet retain their lordships. Ashcroft is still to declare his tax status.

The melange of actors, business men and politicians produces sycophants not saints.

In what orifice resides the nobility supposed to be inherent in knighthoods and lordships?

David Hare, supposedly a scourge of the establishment, whose plays expose the peccadilloes and corruptions of the establishment, swallows down his knighthood and all those seeking approbation follow on: McKellen, Kingsley, "Call me Sir Ben, you peasants,"

What of The Dames, Dench, Smith, and Atkins.

Hopkins grabs his title and then takes American citizenship.

Melvyn Bragg says he is only taking his peerage so he can help abolish the Lords. Lordy, lordy Melv darling how long, how long? Your fabled hair will have fallen out long before Lords reform takes place, if it ever does.

Peter "Mandy" Mandelson, knobbled twice for less than straightforward behaviour whilst in office. A man utterly without principles, badly lacking in political and moral judgement is rewarded with a highly paid job in Europe and a Lordship and brought back by the infantile Gordon Brown to sort out a crisis. He fails at that too. He has now crept away to make more money in business circles using his failed judgement to advise others. John Prescott, the last of the working class socialists, man of the people, one of the few politicians to have had a real job, a serial bonker and master of the left jab, dribbles his thanks for his "enoblement," without a backward glance at his Labour heritage. What has shocked me more than most is the award to the fraudster Gerald Ronson of a CBE for services to charity.

When caught red-handed with his hand in the till, the property tycoon and devoted father of four girls, went to prison for one year and was fined £5 million pounds, at the time the largest fine handed down by a British criminal court.

He was greeted after serving only six months with a present from his fragrant wife of a £47,000 Porsche. He later claimed that the prosecution was "anti-Semitic", and "the British justice system moved the goal posts to send me to prison."

The line stretches out to the crack of doom and all bend the knee, touch the forelock and get a good table at a restaurant.

What are the character and qualities a knight or lord should have according to the ancients? A knight errant was supposed to be a man of chivalrous, adventurous, quixotic nature, intervening on behalf of the threatened and weak.

St Martin of Tours tore his knightly cloak and gave half to a freezing beggar.

The virtues of a knight, the ancient books tell us were the seven considered qualities needed by the true knight; the Courage to fight when outnumbered and wounded and never to bend the knee to evil opponents.

Justice, the justice of Solomon, dispensed without fear or favour.

Mercy, a generous quality of forgiveness granted to the mistaken and wayward. Generosity, a literal and metaphysical concept; giving alms to those in need and be magnanimous to those who fall short of the highest principles.

Faith, the trust and integrity typified by a knight in shining armour.

Nobility, which is to uphold one's convictions at all times, especially when unobserved and help to inspire those around you.

Impossible to fulfil all those demands, I know, but I wonder how many of our public figures ever think or act in any of those terms.

A knight of the Shire is a Conservative politician knighted for services to the party. Tainted money buys the ermine, smoothes the passage to the high table, placates potential rebels and gives influence to sordid and shameful characters strutting about the corridors of power. A Prince of the realm attends abroad as a special representative of Britain.

He gets £250,000 pounds a year from Mummy. The cost of his trips and expenses averages £4000 pounds a week. This includes such matters of public importance as £2,000 pounds for a helicopter to take him from Windsor to Deal for an hour spent at a golf drinks party, £11,148 to the golf links in Ayrshire for a presentation.

This is a man cushioned and protected from the real world who can say "bankers should not be demonised because bonuses in the scheme of things are minute."

Like his brain. His equally brain-deficient ex-wife Sarah Ferguson who used his name to raise money for a tabloid exposure said recently;

"Andrew is a great man and a thoroughly good person… he's a model boy (He's fifty for heaven's sake). He doesn't drink, he goes to bed early." You can't make it up.

The Daily Mail readers and others of that ilk suck up to these leeches. Their leading columnist, Melanie Phillips, a mendacious lady who threshes and writhes in the gutter press and on the radio programme called The Moral Maze, spews out her hatred of the working classes, lambasts Social security "cheats" but has no problem with Cayman Island and Jersey tax avoiders or newspaper proprietors who pay no tax in Britain like the "Dirty Digger," and The Barclay brothers.

My hit list includes David Aaronovitch, a skilled sophist and Zionist sympathiser now writing for the Times and The Jewish Chronicle. This leading commentator in British public life, in an exchange of emails on Twitter tried to smear me with anti-Semitism, but didn't have the guts to go the whole way. Then when I asked him what his position was on the Israeli Supreme Court decision to ban Palestinians who marry Israelis from gaining Israel citizenship, his response was

"There is no reason other than in your world why a British Half Jewish (sic) journalist "must" know about an Israeli Court decision."

What's being half Jewish got to do with the question ?

He never did answer the question and told me to "get lost."

I replied "I thought you would never ask."

He is now busy trying to make a case for going to war with Iran, apparently forgetting his rabble rousing non-combatant role in the debacle of Iraq which he vehemently supported from the side-lines with his neo-con American and British friends.

Many more thousands must die in bloody battle and sectarian violence in the villages, towns, deserts and mountains of Iraq and Afghanistan before he and his colleague Danny Finklestein's blood lust is satisfied.

Nick Cohen is another dissembler, though he is more in the liberal closet when writing for the Observer. Geoffrey Alderman, a regular contributor to the Jewish Chronicle, is a supreme practitioner of casuistry, a specious misleader of the truth.

I needed this rant, but I know it is useless. The right will win most battles whilst a supine opposition wrings its hands.

Let's think about real heroes and decent people.

A group of terrorists detonate a bomb on the London Underground.

Through the dust and devastation come knights in shining armour.

PC David Hill paused for a second at the mouth of the underground tunnel thinking of a second bomb and then plunged into the dark unknown.

At the inquest he was asked why he did that: "Because I was there."

His fellow heroes all downplayed their courage and heroism.

Steve Hucklesby who jumped into a darkened carriage through a broken window to reach the injured, told the inquest he didn't like the term "heroically."

Wing Commander Craig Stanforth said he had been "unfazed", and Jason Rennie who saved the life of a very severely injured passenger, described his actions in calm precise language.

"I used a tourniquet to stem the flow of blood and kept him conscious until the medics arrived. I just figured it would be better to stay with him until it was time for him to go out." Brett Darsley, a firefighter said that when an officer told him and a colleague that there could be further damage, they, "Shrugged their shoulders and carried on." Adrian Heili told his fellow passengers as the carriage filled with noxious smoke to cover their mouths. He then followed the cries of Danny Biddle who lost legs, an eye and his spleen. "I noticed he was missing a leg and blood was coming out of his femoral artery which I closed with my thumb and finger."

Lady Justice Hallet told Steve Hucklesby "You may not like the word heroic but I'm sorry, you are going to have to forgive me. I have to use it because I can't find any other word to describe what you did."

Neither can I.

I am overwhelmed with tears when I contemplate these true, parfit and gentle knights. Surely Her Majesty The Queen must feel her gorge rise and cheeks become inflamed when yet another actor or business person dressed like a tailor's dummy presents him or herself for enoblement, whilst real heroes go back to their ordinary lives, sometimes with, if they are lucky, a medal . The poor lady doesn't know much about nobility, given her dysfunctional family, corrupt governments and attendant sycophants but surely as she dubs the laundered and coiffured hordes shuffling towards her, she is tempted to carry on and swish the sword through their blubbery necks.

O tempes! O mores!

Part Eight

St Anthony's Fire

I woke up with a sense of impending doom on my birthday. I had been to see Wilson to discuss the Marathon. We had a very intense talk about the future.

Wilson told me that things weren't going so well in Heaven. God's foundations were being rocked by internal dissension from Big J and his supporters. Big J was pressing for God to step down and let Big J and the modernisers take over. Unless the truth was broken to the Earth that God was not omnipotent and there were other Galaxies with ambitions to sort out the mess of Earth, then the miasma of horror, genocide, starvation and disease would eventually overwhelm the Earth and destroy it.

The pace of change was painfully slow. One committee on medical ethics under the chairmanship of Galen had been sitting for three hundred years. As for modern Israel the portents were ominous. The Ashkenazim bias against the Sephardim by early leaders like Ben Gurion and Jabotinsky had never really dissipated.

The cabinet, the Army, big business were still largely dominated by Ashkenazim.

Big J was especially infuriated with the activities of fanatics over the future of the Temple Mount in Jerusalem. A group of settlers' aided by Gush Emunim, an extreme movement had planned to blow up the Temple Mount. Even the Israelis knew this would have been disastrous and the plot was foiled by Shin Bet.

But now the war drums were beating again amongst the Likud and Big J forecast a Holocaust if Iran was attacked by Israel.

He understood the dream of many for a perfect kingdom where God ruled in peace and plenty. The huge problem was the ignorance and nonsense spouted by the Tea Party and mostly by American fundamentalist writers and preachers.

Pastor Chuck Smith has a membership of twelve thousand families in his Southern California area and a franchise of born again Christians across America.

Smith asks on his publicity tape "Why God would want to us here on this rotten earth any longer than necessary?"

He quotes the Book of Revelation and Ezekiel where he claims that the prophesy of the rebirth of the nation of Israel and an invasion by Muslims was fulfilled by the 1967 war and the reoccupation of the Temple Mount. A ghastly man called Hal Lindsey whom I had met in Britain and taken on a Religious tour was a four times married ex tug boat captain on the Mississippi River who claimed one had to read the Bible literally.

He wrote a book called *The Late Great Planet Earth* which claimed we were living in the last days which by the end of the nineties had sold over thirty four million copies and been translated into fifty four languages. He has a TV show and regularly takes groups to the Temple Mount and spouts end of day's doctrine interpreting the Bible as facts. His brain dead followers aver that for the Good Times to roll, The Jews have to go through genocide. Jerry Falwell is "awfully sorry" about it but is unequivocal that the Anti-Christ will be Jewish. Meanwhile the Israeli authorities expelled Ezekiel and Abraham and kept a watchful eye on three Virgin Marys walking the streets of Jerusalem as well as the original Twelve Disciples from Milwaukee holding hands and looking rather lost. Every year over one hundred people are admitted to a Jerusalem psychiatric hospital "suffering" from "Jerusalem Syndrome."

The patients have included one middle aged American who had been working out with weights for over two years to build up his strength, convinced he was a reincarnation of Samson and that the Wailing or Western Wall needed pulling down. He had carefully cultivated a mass of natural dark curls and took extreme precautions against going near a barber shop or any person he saw with a pair of scissors.

This had led to a confrontation with a nurse cutting off a bandage of a patient in his ward. Then a foolish doctor told him he wasn't Samson so in a fit of pique he jumped through a closed window, leaving splinters of glass and a trail of blood staining the floors of the hospital.

He was finally detained while trying to pull down a bus stop, and a more sensible and kindly nurse told him he looked exactly like Samson and for all she knew he might be him and she wasn't trying to cut his hair off.

This pacified him and he went home in a happy mood to Pennsylvania and his six children.

One elderly Virgin Mary invited everyone to the birthday of her son Jesus on the Mount of Olives and kept pouring out water from old petrol cans in the hope the water would turn into wine. Israeli Tour Guides have learnt to look out for the symptoms of the Syndrome. Nail biting tourists consumed with anxiety pull a white sheet from their rucksacks and drape it over themselves. From this point there is no stopping them. There is always a competing group of John The Baptist's intoning,

"Prepare ye the way of the Lord" as they prowl the streets in animal skins.

Big J and his advisers were aware that many of The Tea Party politicians of America were convinced they had been sent by God and their electors to bring down Washington.

The rise and rise of Fox News displayed a really ugly side of conservatism.

The Zionist Israeli lobby lied and lied to preserve the status quo and convince the gullible American public to keep approving millions of dollars of aid and arms to Israel, whilst thousands of Palestinians festered in refugee camps and felt like prisoners behind Apartheid walls.

Wilson was quite clearly concerned about his future, whether his eternal life was under threat and whether a battle of the Angels might ensue from the dispute.

He had heard that St Michael was itching for a fight.

He told me, given the situation, that he wasn't sure whether I would be able to go back to Heaven for visits. Wilson said I must be Job-like and weather whatever storms were to come; as he intended to do. We hugged each other and vowed to be stoic and preserve our friendship. As I looked at this green and pleasant land from the carriage windows on my way back to London, and listened to a group of nearly incoherent football fans spewing out foul opinions on anything from the size of their penises, to the big tits of a girl trapped in the same carriage, it was hard to be optimistic.

I wondered why anything should happen to me now. However long I had to go, I was feeling the best was yet to come

After my last visit to the Galaxy I had left buoyed up by the prospects of The Marathon run with Pheidippides, Wilson and Blessing.

My chats with Big J had been inspiring and in some ways tumultuous.

I felt reborn with a new perspective on life and its hopes and expectations.

Yet the perilous and mysterious journey I have tried to convey in these pages, my foolish dreams and brave excursions into new realms entered into an unstoppable spiral of illness and depression. I became viciously cynical, shooting out barbed words that betrayed a self-loathing. My entire sporting prowess deserted me, any remaining dreams evaporated.

The long nightmare started with a small reddish spot on my wrist which I noticed the evening before my birthday. By morning as I lay sipping tea and scratching Rosie's head, it had spread from the base of my thumb to the middle of my wrist.

This was the pattern for the next nine months. The spots would start on my legs, on my thighs, more and more on my bottom, my neck; even my penis didn't escape the onslaught.

They turned into gangrenous looking giant sores, leaking copious amounts of pus needing constant dressing, and were excruciatingly painful.

No doctor or specialist had a solution; their only resort was to radiation, creams and pills and sympathetic sighs. One South African specialist took one look and gasped "Oh Jesus."

I wish. He was not on-call and anyway unable to do anything.

I was suspicious of Big J, Wilson, Blessing, and crucified my family with my searing anger and outbursts of foul language, the tears cascading down my cheeks as I screamed at them. One doctor came up with a name for my disease

"Lymphmatoid Papulosis." He was the only one who knew what it meant but never really enlightened me. I used to yell the phrase at passers-by and in the hospital corridors at the nurses or on the bus, "I've got fucking Lymphmatoid fucking Papulosis."

I could find no solace in anything, even red wine lost its taste and food was anodyne, whatever we tried.

The illness reached a crisis of massive proportions. I was on my way home on the Tube from another session of radiation at St John's Hospital for Skin Diseases in Soho, stuffed with drugs and inwardly weeping. A group of school children stared at me as I whimpered like a beaten dog. I started to hallucinate, writhing in agony like Saint Sebastian as the arrows were fired into his body by the soldiers.

I felt a terrible burning sensation in all my limbs.

The next thing I knew I was vomiting into a bowl at St Georges Hospital in Tooting as painful muscular contractions wracked my body. I know now I went into a coma, and was taken home, at K's insistence to be nursed by her and Blessing.

They both knew if I was going to die, I wanted to die at home in my own bed and surroundings. The surreal atmosphere was exacerbated by the fact that I could hear Blessing and K, my daughters and friends talking about me and the illness but was unable to let them know I was listening and wasn't going to give up.

Karen shared my love of music and developed a theory that I could be helped by heavy doses of Leonard Cohen, Verdi, Mozart, and Chopin. So every day she would play something by them from my awakening to the time I drifted into a semblance of sleep, though it was hard for them to tell the difference from the coma or whether I was sleeping.

One day, I had no way of knowing what day it was, Blessing was reading to Karen.

In the background I could hear Tito Gobbi singing *Di Provenza al Mar* from *La Traviata*, an aria that had always touched me.

"I found this in a book from my mother's collection. The monks of the Order of St Anthony in the middle ages were known for treating a condition of bewitchment, symptoms of which were crawling fiery sensations in the skin, tingling in the fingers, tinnitus, hallucinations, mania, melancholia, and delirium. Patients often went into a coma. The monks had some success in alleviating and often curing the disease.

"Who was St Anthony?" asked Karen.

St Anthony was considered to be the first hermit and the founder of monasticism.

The story goes that he heard one day, a sermon in which the speaker exhorted his congregation; *"If thou wilt be perfect go and sell all thou hast."*

He lived in an abandoned fort for twenty years without looking on the face of man. He lived in c.251 to 356AD in the mountain area of the Eastern Desert between the Nile and the Red Sea, where the monastery of Der Mar Antonius still stands. His represented image in the following centuries was of a man standing in a flaming fire, symbolical of the disease his name is associated with, St Anthony's Fire, the red fiery infection, that was often the first sign of the illness."

I could hear the excitement in Karen's voice.

"What was the cause, what was the cure?"

Blessing said, "Hold on, hold on. It wasn't until the seventeenth century that a connection was made between an infected type of rye and weather conditions."

Early research by the Frenchman Denis Dodart after a mysterious outbreak in the area of the Limousin led to the phenomenon being called Ergotism, a condition caused by the ingestion of ergots which are highly toxic. Ergot tainted rye was believed to have been the cause of the outbreaks of hysteria in the Salem Witch Trials immortalised by Arthur Miller in his play *The Crucible*. As a result of reading Sheila's book, Blessing started serious research. She discovered an outbreak in August 1951 in Pont St Esprit in France where one in twenty of the inhabitants went apparently mad, writhing in agony and with burning sensations in their limbs.

It was quickly diagnosed as "Bread Rye" poisoning. Blessing went to *Pont Esprit* "Bridge Of The Holy Spirit" and tracked down the local retired doctor who had treated most of the afflicted. On her return she and Karen tracked down a specialist who was prepared to try and help.

Dr Shaheed was a Palestinian exiled from his beloved land because of political activism. I could hear his calm voice as he spoke to me as if he knew I could hear and understand. He explained it would take a combination of vasodilators, anti-coagulates, low molecular weight dextras and a "sympathetic bronchial plexus" plus possibly Diazepam for any convulsions. Of course I had no idea what he was talking about but for the first time I felt hope. After the beginning of the treatment everybody got very excited when I tapped a finger to Cohen singing,

"And the women tore their blouses off and the men they danced on the polka dots."

We will never know how I contracted the disease. I did indeed eat a lot of Rye bread but had I been living in a combination of moist weather, cool temperatures and delayed harvests?

No, Dr Shaheed didn't think so, but a series of injections made me feel better.

Each day I got stronger and indicated I was aware of them all.

As Leonard Cohen sang;

"The wars they will be fought again,
The holy dove it will be caught again, bought and sold and caught again, the dove is never free
Ring the bells that still can ring.
Forget your perfect offering
There's a crack, a crack in everything, that's how the light gets in
That's how the light gets in."

I sat up for the first time in nine months and wept like a baby.

Karen, Blessing, the girls, the doctors, all were euphoric at my recovery.

It was a kind of miracle I suppose. I walked on Wimbledon Common, went to

Painshill Park and London Wetlands with Karen and Blessing and our new friend the Doctor Shaheed.

In my mind I made plans to run the scheduled marathon.

When I did confess my plans, the cries of protest from friends and family were loud. But Karen and Blessing understood.

A second chance means something. Maybe Big J had tried to help after all.

I had to do it. I contacted Wilson and Blessing and I went to the cave.

I had taken Karen into my secret world and she understood at once.

"You will come back?"

Boulogne Sur Mer

We discussed extensively the matter of a training location. We wanted to be away from any pressures. The only people who knew we were going to do the run were Up There. I had been visiting Boulogne for fifty years. My sister Susan, as a young girl had run off with a Frenchman, over twenty years her senior from the region and had four children and numerous grandchildren.

The marriage hadn't survived and she was now married to a German patent judge from Munich, Heiner. To strangers the relationship had seemed an odd one.

For twenty years Heiner had lived and worked in Munich and driven eight hundred miles every three weeks or so to visit Susan in Boulogne. He was now retired and they lived together, devoted to two brown Labradors, Paddy and Sam and of course to each other. I have always been close to Susan and the Frenchies who multiply by the hundreds every year. Nephews, nieces, great nephews and great nieces, even a great great nephew. I cherish the family gatherings under oaks and amongst flowers, sipping Champagne and St Emilion and choosing from a cheese board of dozens of varieties.

Heiner is a charming and equable man loved by all the family.

Boulogne doesn't yield up its charms on first acquaintance.

The British Air Force destroyed much of the harbour and surrounding area to suppress German Naval activity following D Day in 1944. The rebuilding was in Brutalist style, reminiscent of Centre Point in London.

My sister lives in the Old Town in a beautiful eighteenth century house with a walled garden on the Ramparts. The streets are mostly cobbled and there are four narrow gates for entry. On the Ramparts are a 13th century castle, at one time a prison and now a museum. The nineteenth century Basilica has an enormous crypt and the second largest dome in Europe after St Peter's in Rome.

The real attraction of Boulogne for me lies in its countryside and coast line. Within minutes from its centre are woods, forests and chateaux.

One can arrive at the beach by walking through a verdant forest over hillocks of grass, mounds of sand and wild flowers. As we crest the rise, my spirits soar. There waiting expectantly for me is the sea and a horizon stretching to England, dotted with sail boats and the occasional ferry. The long and seemingly endless beach is an incitement to the dogs, who are so excited, and rush down to plunge into the sea. It is a sparsely populated beach but there are some people on horseback or riding wind cycles on the sand. Joggers jog without any of the usual symptoms of stress one sees on the streets of London. The wind, sun and open space give off great whiffs of freedom, of movement and there is no need to strain, grimace and sweat ferociously. Dogs should be kept on leads but this rule is often ignored. Giant seagulls without any fear strut along the shore with puffed out chests like bouncers outside a night club, contrasting with the sand plovers delicate bodies, and balletic movements.

The groups of plovers flirt with the waves, teasing them, and then nipping briefly into the last of the wave before coyly retreating in an elegant sideways quick step as if on points for the dance of the swans in Swan Lake.

My sister found a house close to the beach we could rent for a month.

Wilson was put in charge of training and diet. We rose at dawn and ran for several miles along the cliff top. We then plunged into the cold sea and swam for an hour. Back for breakfast and a sleep. Then we ran more miles in the afternoon, this time across the dunes and through the woodland. After early supper we then held long talks about the task that faced Blessing and me. For Wilson the marathon run was like a walk in the park.

We talked about the limits to human endurance in sport.

Usain Bolt had burst onto the sprinting track at the Beijing Olympics, becoming the first man to go under 9.7seconds. He then, a year later, went to 9.58. The experts pondered and worked out that in 1896 athletes were performing at 75% of their potential whilst in 2008 it was 99%. Bolt had astonished the world by slowing down to wave at the crowd as he crossed the line. One expert asserts that the brain is the deciding factor in going fast but is unable to process signals fast enough.

Wilson said he thought it was too early to know if Bolt could go faster.

The engaging Michael Johnson, 400m record holder and now a commentator for the BBC pointed out, as he saw it, technical flaws in Bolt, claiming he lost power by moving too much from side to side. But Wilson argued that when Bolt's left foot is on the ground he rocks to the right and when his right foot is on the ground he rocks to the left and he is perfectly balanced. Wilson also thought that Bolt was physically different from most modern sprinters who are strength-based and he was unusually tall. "Now let's look at marathon runners. Haile Gebrselassie ran a 2 hour 3minutes 59 seconds race. In 2008 Sammy Wanjiru ran 2 hours 06.32 in Beijing in sticky and oppressive conditions.

"He was only twenty one" I said.

"Yes, Hailie's thirty seven now but still holds the world record at 2 hours 03.59.

I think he or someone else will do under two hours soon.

The best runners know how to conserve their energy; the ideal is to expend 30% less energy than your competitors."

Wilson shrewdly varied our training with physical games on the beach and handicapping us, making us carry bags of stones and running with one leg tied to the other person's leg.

We also visited some of the delightful little villages along the coast.

Many of the beaches have great lumps of twisted metal and concrete, dying imperceptible deaths, sinking into the sand, the remnants of the bunkers built in World War II to repel the Germans. One of the saddest reminders of the war is The Jew's Walk, built by Jewish prisoners, many of whom ended up in concentration camps, a constant reminder of the Vichy Government's collaboration with the Nazis in transporting Jews to the camps. France has never come to terms with the anti- Semitic and subservient Vichy era or indeed the Algerian debacle.

The training was tough and in the last week we ran two marathons, Wilson romping home a long way in front. Blessing is now grey haired like me but still looks much younger than her years. She has an elegant running style, loping along like a cheetah, disciplined and running within her strength. I am ancient, grey and overweight, with tits. He who indulges bulges. No amount of dieting or running could shift my substantial breasts. Blessing and Wilson advised me to wear a sports bra, humiliating, but I did feel much more comfortable wearing one of Blessings' pink numbers.

I just hoped no-one would find out. Whilst I envied Wilson's and Blessing's apparent effortless styles, I had to accept I was not going to become like them in a few weeks, if ever. Zen philosophy advises one to make peace with your pace. I spent the first few days breaking in my running shoes and testing a variety of socks. Even Wilson advised a running hat given the heat of Greece in the spring. My feet were a problem, almost permanently cracked skin on the soles of my feet and two toes that burnt like fire after even short walks. I rubbed Vaseline and other oils into the cracks and Wilson massaged the toes with some successful effects. Blessing was concerned for me and rubbed my aching muscles with firm and strong hands. They were both pleased with our training but worried about my ability to finish.

We talked about my Wimbledon win and my exploits for England at Wembley but I was a lot older now. We had a conference. We were going to carry our water on our backs with a tube to our mouths. Wilson and Blessing thought I should not even attempt a respectable time but run within my capabilities. Wilson gave me a mantra "Pace and a Peaceful mind." "You can do this but a lot will depend on your mind, the thoughts you marshall as you trot along.

Forget about the rules, they are there to be confounded."

On the last night we had a celebratory dinner and some wine in our compact kitchen. We had all decided we would bring our favourite treat to the party.

It was then we found out Wilson's guilty secret; Jaffa Cakes. Yes the iron man, our hero had an Achilles heel. For those of you ignorant of this elixir for the stomach, a Jaffa Cake is a sponge biscuit with an orange flavoured jelly filling and chocolate topping. We devoured it and then engaged in a discussion of its merits.

Is it a cake or a biscuit?

When fresh it has a soft taste which turns hard when stale, when it is permitted to dunk it in your cup of tea. Blessing and I both shared a passion bordering on mania for Cadbury Fruit and Nut Chocolate. It was impossible for either of us to leave the tiniest piece of an opened bar. An unopened one would sit for about ten seconds on the table before one of us grabbed the bar and started tearing the cover off.

So we agreed that Blessing would provide the chocolate and I would bring to the table Vieux Boulogne, a cheese which bears the title of the smelliest cheese in the world.

It is soft and elastic with a central pate surrounded by moist red orange washed rind and is washed in beer during its production.

We wrapped our arms around each other, wept a little and roared "Athens or Death."

The Marathon

*"We are different in essence from other men.
If you want to win something, run 100 meters.
If you want to experience something run a marathon."*
Emil Zatopek

*"I always loved running, you could do it yourself,
go in any direction fast or slow fighting the wind,
seeking new sights just on the strength of your feet
and the courage of your lungs."*
Paula Radcliffe

Two months later in April we stood waiting at Mount Penteli for Pheidippides.

He suddenly appeared looking super fit, bronzed and slim.

We agreed that he would lead us so we would take the correct route.

Kindly no-one suggested that I might get out of sight.

However, Blessing discreetly slipped me a map.

We looked at each other, shook hands and at a signal from Pheidippides we set off.

It was very warm but a little breeze wafted across my face.

I remember that day as the greatest day of my life. It was a gentle slope uphill westwards as Pheidippides had promised. As I ran uttering my mantra, my life spread out before me, the triumphs, the failures, the tears, recriminations, the misunderstandings never resolved.

Lordy lordy sometimes we stumble, sometimes we fall. We hear the thundering of the Gods in the heavens, accompanied by the angel's echoing songs of distress and grief until the sweet hour of prayer enters our soul and we are whole again.

I saw the group ahead slowing down but waved them on. The smell of fennel and thyme wafted in my nostrils. My feet felt fine, my breathing, although laboured on the uphill, soon recovered on the down slopes. "Peace and a peaceful mind" was what I felt. The world was suddenly benign and my optimism for its future was so intense I felt I was flying. Glancing at the map I realised that incredibly I was approaching the final run down into Athens. As I came around a rocky corner, Pheidippides, Blessing and Wilson were running almost at a standstill.

I came alongside and we ran abreast holding hands into Athens shouting to bemused citizens "The victory is ours."

We sat in a cafe in sight of the Acropolis. We drank Retsina and ate calamari, whitebait, and Greek salad. Gentle laughter and profound silences echoed into the early hours.

We felt a sense of closure but other possibilities in the future broke into our conversation and thoughts. Pheidippides took his leave. We hugged and promised to keep in touch having no idea whether that would be possible.

Pheidippides walked down the street in that lithe athletic walk of his we had come to relish and which I had tried to imitate.

He stopped at the corner, turned and waved and was gone.

We had arranged for our luggage to be sent to a hotel in Athens and repaired there for blissful sleep with dreams of the special light and contours of Greece floating through my mind.

Epilogue

Where to Next?
Who Wants To Know?

"Look Homeward Angel"
"One's country is wherever it is well with one".
John Milton

My back is too chronic to answer any more calls from either the Football or Cricket teams. There is talk of my lighting the Olympic flame at the 2012 Olympics in London. We shall see. I take my diabetic pill, my atrial fibrillation pills, and my blood pressure pills. Go to the osteopath, do the exercises, wear the special sandals my daughters bought me, grimace as I pull myself out of the chair and stagger towards the wine rack. When I was young my life seemed like a fast running mountain stream furiously tossing aside the boulders, stones and pebbles in my way, clinging temporarily to logs and trees until swept along to new horizons and adventures.

Now it seems like a grinding stone in a grain store,
"where snares and pits and traps and webs do lie."
And I am the huckster of my own wavering thoughts.
Roll up! Roll up! The Circus has come to town. I'm cracking the whip.
The lions bare their teeth. They prowl around me balefully licking their lips.
Listen to me, I cry. Even as I start the litany of so-called achievements I am boring myself.

The compensations are my family and friends.

I suppose like most of us, I sought love as a young man.

The chances of finding it with Karen over 45 years ago must be millions to one.

But we found it, snipped and snarled, cut and slashed at its foundations, eventually recognising the precious nature of what we had achieved. We clung on to each other so we wouldn't drown and our love and friendship has deepened with the years.

My daughters Sophie and Tessa have been difficult, cantankerous, menstrual, feisty, a stimulation, a light, a joy, a pleasure and always loving and loved. They keep us going.

As ever, the garden, wine, music, reading, writing and the cats are my solace and joy.

I walk in fields of wonder. Painshill Park, Virginia Water, Richmond Park and Wimbledon Common. I read about ten books a month, mostly from the London Library, make trips to Museums and The Riverside in Fulham to see a bargain film double bill.

Cohen, Springsteen, Simon, Miles, Bird, Barber, Colyer, Kiri ti Kanawa, Don Carlos, Chopin, are all just part of the interior life I lead.

I stay curious.

There will be those who will start to read this book and who won't get it.

My nephew Roger will, even though many of the sports people are before his time. Roger shares with me a deep love of sport.

He knows the depths and the heights of watching England play football or cricket.

Roger is the worst person in the world with whom to watch a football match.

Whitefaced and fidgety when England went five to one up against the Germans with ten minutes to go, Roger cautioned, "They can still come back."

And of course there is a great phalanx of sports nuts who will know of what I dream, of what I conjure up to enrich my daily musings. They too have scored centuries and hat tricks for their country, were there when Johnny Wilkinson dropped the goal to win the Rugby World Cup, were at Lords for a Botham century, swear they were at Wembley for England's football World Cup win in 1966, at Wimbledon for the lengthy Pancho Gonzales and Charlie Pasarell contest before the introduction of the tie break, Borg and McEnroe epics and the stupendous Federer and Nadal final.

Finally I wasn't going to reveal the following, out of modesty, or fear of publicity and because I am a Republican at heart. As I get older I go further politically to the left but I revere in chivalrous and noble behaviour as I described the people's actions in the Tube bomb atrocity. I have ranted and raved against the privileged, the phonies and the titled in our society. But what happened was so unexpected.

That doesn't make it right but you won't see me use my title on the cover of the book or on my letterheads. You won't hear me talk about it to anyone and most of my family and friends still don't know.

The truth, the whole truth must come out one day, probably when I'm dead and it is best it is written by my pen now. So here goes.

A little while ago I was in the Mall quite early on my way to the London Library in St James Square.

A Rolls Royce was passing as I crossed the road.

It stopped and the window was wound down.

The Queen put her head out "How are you Ricky?

Scoring many goals these days?"

As I started to reply I heard a heavy footfall and turned to see a huge man coming at the car with a gun in one hand. He pointed it at Her Majesty. I dropped my book bag and smashed my hand down on his outstretched gun hand and then struck him with all my strength in the side of the face. He fell to the ground and within seconds we were surrounded by security men with guns and policemen.

The man was handcuffed and pinned to the ground. I stood there panting and nursing my hand. Suddenly the security men parted and the Queen came through the gap followed by her equerry in gold braid.

He drew his sword from its scabbard and I felt a momentary fear.

But he presented it to the Queen.

She took it, judged its weight and said, "Kneel Ricky."

On trembling knees I knelt on the red pavement.

She tapped me lightly on both shoulders.

"I dub thee Knight for the noble services of Chivalry and Courage for your Queen.

Arise, Sir Ricky."

Printed in Great Britain
by Amazon.co.uk, Ltd.,
Marston Gate.